Worship Refocused

How To Become The Worshiper The Father Is Seeking

David Miles

ISBN 978-93-5610-452-5

Published in India 2022 by Pencil

A brand of
One Point Six Technologies Pvt. Ltd.
123, Building J2, Shram Seva Premises,
Wadala Truck Terminal, Wadala (E)
Mumbai 400037, Maharashtra, INDIA
E connect@thepencilapp.com
W www.thepencilapp.com

CONTENTS

Endorsements

This page intentionally left blank

1. Where This Began

So here is yet another book on Worship!

There is a prolific, daunting and perhaps somewhat confusing array of books on this topic in every Christian bookstore. And therefore, why the need for another?

I first started leading church music groups in 1976, and for the next 30 years was very much involved in many different types of church music as a musician and as a leader.

Mty love of music started with my mother who was professionally trained in voice and piano, at the Melbourne Conservatorium of Music.
Our home was always full of music and I learned to play piano at a young age. Then in the 1960's I announced I wanted to learn guitar, much to my parents horror. However, Dad said that if I learned to play guitar, he would buy me one. So I borrowed a guitar from a friend and learned to play that thing in a few weeks.

I was part of a folk group in high school, and we practiced a lot and performed a lot too. So later after I was married and my wife, Alison, and I became part of a very alive Charismatic Church in Sydney, it was a logical thing for me to join the music team.

That was near the beginning of the "modern" chorus and praise and worship songs era. They were exciting, fresh and inspiring songs and choruses. Many of the songs and choruses we sang then were straight out of the Scripture, and so we learned a lot Scripture (the Psalms in particular) that way.
There was also at this time, a new phenomenon in music. The development of Christian recording artists. Amy Grant, Keith Green, Larry Norman, The Imperials, and so many more, who left an indelible impression on modern Christian music.

As the years progressed, there gradually arose a new industry around Christian music that has now become a major commercial venture for some, fuelled by skilful producers and marketers.

Alongside this Christian stream of music, was a secular stream that captured the attention of the younger generation, and also proved to be very lucrative.
In order to compete for the youth, the Church started to absorb secular music styles, production and ideas. This

mixture became slowly accepted in the Church and gradually led to a shift away from the purity of music, and the gift, and its purpose as described in Scripture.

This book seeks to describe that shift, and to come back to the Scriptures for the original perspective and understanding that worship, and praise should rightly occupy in our lives.

A major part of this shift was the association of the word "praise" with the word "worship". It began in the mid '60's and early 70's.
Before that, praise was not necessarily associated with worship.

We have all heard of a praise and worship session. Usually that means a few up-tempo songs known as praise, followed by some slower, devotional songs which are considered to be worship. The experienced worship leader knows how to read the audience and when to move from praise to worship, for maximum effect.
The tech crew also knows how to follow the mood, with lighting and visual effects.

This is known almost universally as praise and worship and is now an established musical genre.

But praise is fundamentally different from worship, as we will see. The long-standing association of those two words makes it very difficult to separate one from the other, but it is vitally important that we come back to the Scripture for our understanding and definitions of worship and of praise.

Because of the wrong coupling of these words together, it is an automatic assumption that praise and worship is what happens at the beginning of a church service. As a result, many believers actually do not know what worship really is.
Worship is as different from praise, as temperature is from direction.

As we travel the Scriptures together on this topic, we will find that the worship which God desires, and the worshipers He seeks, are not the expressions we usually see in the Church today.

We will also find that what we consider to be praise, is a long way short of how the Bible describes praise, and that our praise has become diluted and focused almost exclusively on music. This is not the Biblical emphasis.

It is also tragic that New Age thinking and practices have become thoroughly embedded in our church music, leading to a distraction from the main thrust of the Gospel and a shift away from its power.

These days, the emotional effects of the "Worship Service" are well documented and the manipulative effects of "Worship Music" are recognised as a powerful tool for indoctrination.

In short, our "worship" has become focused upon something other than that which God intended. In fact, it is not worship at all.
May you be challenged, enriched and truly blessed as we take this journey together.

BA Dip Ed (Inconsequential Man's institution), Masters of Life Experience (School of Hard Knox),
PhD in making mistakes (School of the Holy Spirit)

2. Worship's Importance to the Father

A good place to start, is with what I regard as one of the most important passages in the whole Bible about worship. It tells of the Father's heart regarding worship.

It is found in John Chapter 4, and verses 4-26. (Take a few moments to read this yourself)
Here, Jesus is talking to the Samaritan woman at the well, but he begins by asking her for a drink of water. She soon gains an understanding that Jesus has some very important things to say to her and in fact she realises He is a Prophet, so she asks him about one of the big issues of their day - where to worship.

The Samaritans and the Jews were greatly divided about worship, amongst other things. The Jews thought that the only real place to worship was in Jerusalem at the temple. However, the Samaritans also had their own temple and places of worship, and so they were despised by the Jews as being counterfeit and mixed-race worshipers.[1]
However, Jesus got to the heart of that division and demolished the argument altogether. He stated to the woman at the well, that people are not going to worship

the Father in either Samaria or Jerusalem. In actual fact, the place is not important.

"The hour is now here", Jesus said, "when neither in Samaria or Jerusalem will you worship the Father…the true worshipers will worship the Father in spirit and in truth, because the Father is seeking people like that to worship Him".
(My slight paraphrase of John 4:23)

To understand that the Father Himself is seeking worshipers, is a gigantic revelation.
Becoming a worshiper and being found by the Father, is something that God the Father Himself is actively seeking.
The importance of such a statement from Jesus cannot be overstated.
Here is the heart of the Father, His plainly stated desire.
This provides a focus and a goal for our lives that has eternal consequences, as well as an overwhelming richness in the present life.

It is very motivational that God himself is telling us what He values, and so we should be wanting to enlist in that company. We can be fashioned into the sort of people the Father is looking for.
This is indeed for everyone!
Therefore it is of supreme importance that we understand exactly who and what the Father is looking for. He is seeking worshipers, but what does that actually mean?
It is not possible to achieve something, if we do not know precisely what we are aiming at.

To become a good translator, you must work hard at knowing the languages fluently;
to become a good racing car driver, you need to develop driving skills with a high degree of precision;
to become a great tennis player, you need to train, learn and practice for many hours. There are so many illustrations.

To become a great worshiper, you need to understand exactly what worship is and practice a lot. No one becomes anything by accident, it must be a deliberate focus.
And we need to know what the endpoint looks like, in order to aim for it. There is the old saying that if you aim for nothing, you are sure to hit it.

Jesus said something quite surprising to this woman at the well.
He told her plainly that he was the Messiah.[2]

This is the first time Jesus actually declared this so clearly to anyone, and He was declaring His supreme authority to be speaking these truths to her.
She listened, and we too should be listening with the same attentiveness.

So what really is it that the Father is looking for?
The answer is of course, people who worship Him in spirit and in truth.
It must be something really important if the Father is seeking these people.

Really, really, important.

Essentially, what is worship?
Who exactly are worshipers?
What do worshipers do?
How do I know if I am a worshiper?
Do I want to be one who is sought and found by the Father?

That is the topic of the next few chapters.
We will have a look at worship in the Old Testament, and then explore worship in the New Testament. But I believe we are in for some surprises, and some of these surprises may be uncomfortable.
There were many times when Jesus corrected the Scribes and Pharisees because of their bad doctrine, shallow understanding of the Scriptures, or their tradition and bias. Jesus made them feel uncomfortable, and even at times, rebuked them.[3]
Perhaps as we journey through this topic together, there will be some of those moments for you too.
There were for me when I was first exploring this topic.

Worship is so important, because we need to understand what the Father is seeking. Once we have that understanding, we can set our sights on pursuing that goal with the help of the Holy Spirit.

There are dozens of references to worship in the Old Testament, but strangely on first glance, not so much in the New Testament.
We will see why this is so, and hopefully see that Jesus, our example in everything, actually models worship for us.

The New Testament is a worship manual, powered by the Holy Spirit.

HALLALUJAH!

3. Worship and The Old Testament

Having looked at why we are discussing this topic and how we got here, we are at the beginning of an analysis of what the Bible really says about worship.
What were people in the Old Testament actually doing when they "worshipped"?

One way of doing this, is to dial up all the references to "worship, worshiping, worshipers" in any concordance, and review them all in their context. This is what I have done, and I would invite anyone who has the time, to do the same. It is a remarkable journey and I will summarise some discoveries in the following few paragraphs.

We will find that there are common elements in all the instances of worship mentioned, but I have chosen a few to illustrate some important things we have too frequently overlooked.

Abraham

Let us look first at worship as portrayed by Abraham, when God asked him to sacrifice Isaac.
The story is well known, and can be found in Genesis 22:1-14, if you have not read it yet.
It is an extraordinary example of worship.

Isaac was the son that God promised to give Abraham, so that his offspring (which is Israel) would be so numerous that they could not be counted, and would bless all nations. Then God tested Abraham by asking him to sacrifice Isaac on an altar. Abraham complied with God's request, but when he was about to kill Isaac with the knife, God told him to stop. Then God supplied a ram caught in a bush, for the actual offering.

This story is remarkable on many levels and has much depth and significance, but I want to point out something Abraham said, in verse 5 of Chapter 22 in Genesis.
Abraham had journeyed for three days with his son Isaac, and a couple of servants with a donkey carrying provisions for the journey.
When Abraham reached the place which he knew God had showed him, Abraham said to his servants:

"Stay here with the donkey; I and the boy will go over there and worship, and come again to you".
(Gen 22:5)

Now this is extremely important, because it is the first time worship is mentioned in the Bible.
The principle of "first mention"[4] is of paramount importance, because all of the great themes of the Bible are introduced in Genesis: Salvation, Baptism, The Bride of Christ, The Church, The Second Coming, The Trinity, and as we have just seen, so is Worship. There are other themes and doctrines and they need to be diligently searched out, but it is not the domain of this book to explore all those here.

Notice these four things about this act of worship that Abraham did for the Lord.

First, it seems like Abraham believed God all the way up the mountain, because he says to his servants that he would return with Isaac. Abraham could not have know the outcome, but he trusted God thoroughly and completely. Abraham had determined to obey God and sacrifice Isaac.

Also the New Testament testifies to this:
For what does the Scripture say? "Abraham believed God, and it was counted to him as righteousness." (Romans 4:3)

Second, Isaac observed that there was not an animal for the offering in the things that they carried together, and Isaac believed what his father said.

And Isaac said to his father Abraham, "My father!" And he said, "Here I am, my son." He said, "Behold, the fire and the wood, but where is the lamb for a burnt offering?" Abraham said, "God will provide for himself the lamb for a burnt offering, my son." So they went both of them together. (Genesis 22:7-8)

Third, Isaac submitted willingly to his father, even to the point of being bound on the altar when he could have easily overpowered his father if he wanted. Isaac would have been approximately 20 when they went up this mountain, and Abraham was probably over 120 years old. All this took some time, because Abraham had to build the altar first and I suppose Isaac helped build it.

When they came to the place of which God had told him, Abraham built the altar there and laid the wood in order and bound Isaac his son and laid him on the altar, on top of the wood.
(Genesis 22:9)

Fourth, afterwards, the Lord restated His covenant with Abraham, which was to make his offspring as numerous as the stars in the heavens or the sand on the seashore.

And the angel of the LORD called to Abraham a second time from heaven and said, "By myself I have sworn, declares the LORD, because you have done this and have not withheld your son, your only son, I will surely bless you, and I will surely multiply your offspring as the stars of heaven and as the sand that is on the seashore. And your offspring shall possess the gate of his enemies, and in your offspring shall all the nations of the earth be blessed, because you have obeyed my voice." (Genesis 22:15-18)

The big thing to notice from this story, is that Abraham called sacrificing his son, "an act of worship".

Job

Now let's have a look at one of the oldest heroes of the Scripture, the enigmatic Job.

Job is possibly the oldest book in the Bible, and was written before the Law was given, before the Exodus from Egypt and before the establishment of Israel.

Job is an upright and blameless man who fears God and is highly regarded in his community.

The book is a record of Satan challenging God about Job's uprightness.

Satan tells God that the only reason Job is upright is

because God has protected him.
So Satan challenges God to remove His protection around Job and then see if Job still serves and respects him.

God gives Satan permission to afflict Job, but not to touch Job's life.[5]

Within a very short space of time:[6]
- Job's livestock are stolen by villains who also killed Job's servants.
- Then a firestorm killed all Job's sheep and the shepherds.
- Next, another band of robbers stole all his camels, killing more servants.
- As if that wasn't enough, his 10 children were feasting together in their oldest brother's house when a violent tornado hit the house, destroying it and killing all his children.

Job's reaction to this phenomenal loss is the amazing thing to be noticed.

"Job arose and tore his robe and shaved his head and fell on the ground and worshipped."
(Job 1:21)

What an incredible reaction to this calamity. We don't normally associate worship with tragedy, but this is Job's heart response to the loss of everything.

Job of course had no understanding through the whole drama of what went on "backstage" in the conversation between God and Satan, but his belief and trust in a faithful God never wavered.

Job learned some great and deeper things about God through all this, and at the end, God restored to Job twice as much as he had at the beginning.

Of course there is so much more to the story of Job and many other important lessons to learn from it.

But Job's reaction of worshiping God in the midst of all the loss and suffering, is for now, the important thing to focus on.

King David

No study of worship could ever be complete without mentioning King David.

However at this point, I want to highlight something which is often overlooked about a worship incident in David's life. (You can explore this story in 2 Sam 11:1-27, 12:1-23)

There was a time when this great king, a man described as a "man after God's own heart",[7]committed adultery and murder. It is a tragic story and in the aftermath, David wrote Psalm 51.

But to add to this tragedy, Bathsheba became pregnant and after the baby was born, it became very ill. David sought the Lord for the baby's life with fasting and weeping, but the baby died.

David's reaction is now very startling, as we read in 2 Sam 12:20.

"Then David arose from the earth and washed and anointed himself and changed his clothes. And he went into the house of the Lord and worshiped."

Here again, his response to tragedy, is a response of worship.

David's heart in the midst of trouble, is to worship the Lord.

King Solomon

Now we come to a classic passage on worship, which is highlighted in many teachings about worship. The occasion is described in 2 Chronicles 7:1-10

The event is the dedication of Solomon's Temple, a stunning and majestic building unequalled and unrivalled in even the present world. There are many estimates of how much it would cost to build in today's money, ranging from $5 billion to over $150 Billion.[8]

So when it came to the dedication, there was much ceremony, many animals sacrificed (22,000 oxen and 120,000 sheep), music and fanfare, and a fourteen day feast for all Israel. We are looking at a feast for 3 million people for fourteen days - an extremely large feast!

(1.3 million was the estimated number of men at King David's last census, so 3 million people is probably an underestimate. 2 Samuel 24:9)

Three things to focus on from this passage are that firstly, after Solomon prayed, fire from Heaven consumed the sacrifice and secondly, the Glory of God filled the temple so thickly that the priests could not enter the temple. Quite an amazing sight! Lastly, the people's response was to fall on their faces and worship God, giving Him thanks.

When all the people of Israel saw the fire come down and the glory of the LORD *on the temple, they bowed down with their faces to the ground on the pavement and worshiped and gave thanks to the* LORD, *saying, "For he is good, for his steadfast love endures forever." (2 Chronicles 7:3)*

It is interesting that singing is not mentioned in this passage.

Other Examples

There is another worship example from David's life that should be mentioned here. The incident is when David brought back the Ark of God that the Philistines had captured.

It was a long journey. The Ark had been in the house of a man named Obed-Edom and it was going back to Jerusalem. This distance was somewhere in the vicinity of 12 miles (19 km), but it is is not known with certainty.[9]The distance itself is not so important, except that it was a long journey in those days.
The amazing thing here, is that every 6 steps, they stopped and sacrificed two animals.

And when those who bore the ark of the LORD had gone six steps, he sacrificed an ox and a fattened animal. (2 Samuel 6:13).

Even though the word "worship" is not used in this passage, this is precisely what they were doing, and it was extravagant.

Here's a calculation to ponder.
If we assume the distance travelled, carrying the Ark from Obed-Edom's house to Jerusalem, is 19 km, and the length of six steps is about 4 metres, the total number of stops they made in order to sacrifice is 4,750. Which means they

sacrificed 9,500 animals on this journey.
Whichever way you work it out, it was a lot.

That much sacrifice takes a lot of money, time, many animals, and there would have been a lot of blood. Let us ask some further questions about the logistics involved in a simple statement like 2 Sam 6:13. There could be questions like:

Did they bring all those animals with them and who looked after them all?

How long does it take to sacrifice an ox and a fattened animal?

Did they actually stop and have a feast every six steps?

And just how many people did this whole procession involve?

Also, how much planning and preparation time did all this take?

What about security from marauding raiders?…

We know King David was very wealthy, but with the amount of planning, people and time involved, this is a gargantuan, extravagant occasion of worship.

There are so many other instances of worship mentioned in the Old Testament that it is difficult to choose just a few. However, here are some more examples where worship is mentioned.

It is interesting to note that there is as much encouragement to worship the true God, as there are warnings against worshiping false gods. (About 27 of each, depending on how you classify them).

Here are some exhortations to Israel, to worship the one true God:

Now this man (Hannah's husband) used to go up year by year from his city to worship and to sacrifice to the LORD of hosts at Shiloh, where the two sons of Eli, Hophni and Phinehas, were priests of the LORD.
(1 Samuel 1:3)

Ascribe to the LORD the glory due his name; bring an offering and come before him! Worship the LORD in the splendor of holiness;
(1 Chronicles 16:29)

Oh come, let us worship and bow down; let us kneel before the LORD, our Maker!
(Psalm 95:6)

Worship the LORD in the splendor of holiness; tremble before him, all the earth!
(Psalm 96:9)

Here are some warnings against worshiping other gods:

...for you shall worship no other god, for the LORD, whose name is Jealous, is a jealous God,
(Exodus 34:14)

And if you forget the LORD your God and go after other gods and serve them and worship them, I solemnly warn you today that you shall surely perish.
(Deut 8:19)

But if your heart turns away, and you will not hear, but are drawn away to worship other gods and serve them, I declare to you today, that you shall surely perish. You shall not live long in the land that you are going over the Jordan to enter and possess.
(Deut 30:17-18)

But if you turn aside from following me, you or your children, and do not keep my commandments and my statutes that I have set before you, but go and serve other gods and worship them,
then I will cut off Israel from the land that I have given them, and the house that I have consecrated for my name I will cast out of my sight, and Israel will become a proverb and a byword among all peoples. And this house will become a heap of ruins. Everyone passing by it will be astonished and will hiss, and they will say, 'Why has the LORD done thus to this land and to this house?'
(1 Kings 9:6-8)

Summing up the characteristics of worship in the Old Testament

On looking at examples of people worshiping in the Old Testament, we do see some things which are common to every instance, whether the examples are about worshiping God or about worshiping idols.

These things are common, and at least one or more is present in every act of worship. Occasionally all of them were present.

1. Bowing or prostrating oneself
2. Sacrifice - usually of livestock or produce
3. Offering - of money or time
4. Incense or prayer - usually from the priest
5. Declaration - speaking things out loud

Notice that these 5 characteristics of worship are all actions, and this is an important thing to discover about worship.

Even the name says it all, "an ACT of worship", which implies action or something that must be done.

Worship is a verb.

It is also important to see that the act of worship always involves a focus.

In all cases, because worship involves action, the action is always directed at or to something.

In the case of true worship, the focus is God. In false

worship, or pagan worship (often called worshiping idols), the focus is something man-made.

In the worst case scenario of direct satanic worship, the devil is the deliberate and active focus of the worship. This is what he has always wanted since the beginning of creation. We will talk more about that later.

Let's now progress and have a look at the Psalms, as there are some amazing things to find there about worship.

4. Worship and Praise

In our last Chapter, we looked at some examples of worship in the Old Testament, in the lives of Moses, Job, David and Solomon. We also summarised the major characteristics of worship and saw what people were doing when they worshipped.

Now we come to a topic that has been a source of confusion for a long time in the church.
Stated simply it is this, worship is not the same thing as praise.

One might say, "well, it doesn't really matter because it is all to the Lord", and that is true.
However, the motivating thing for me, is that the Father is seeking worshipers, not praisers. So it is important for us to know the difference between these two expressions in our walk as disciples.

The importance of praise in Scripture cannot be overemphasised. Knowing the difference between worship and praise is essential, but does not diminish the place of praise in our lives. On the contrary, understanding the difference will clarify and reinforce the importance of praise in our daily walk. The Bible has a tremendous amount to say about praise, and our hearts should be filled and continually overflowing with praise.

We have had a look at the defining characteristics of worship in the Old Testament in Chapter 3, so now we will look at the defining characteristics of praise. This will help with our clarification of the difference between worship and praise. It is essential to know the difference, because as we have now seen, the Father is seeking worshipers not praisers.

Some translation considerations

It is essential to know when we look at "praise", what the word actually means in the original Hebrew language.

What actually is praise? What should we be doing?

In a similar way, this also applies to our understanding of our word "love", when translated from the original Greek in the New Testament.

In the Greek language, there are at least 4 words for "love", whereas in English, there is only one. So we need to know as we read the English New Testament, which Greek word was translated "love", in order to understand its full meaning in the Biblical context.

Our translation of the English word "praise" is just like that, because in the Hebrew language, (Old Testament) there are seven distinct words for "praise".
As we understand their definitions, we will see more clearly what it is that God is encouraging us to do when we praise Him.

Here are the seven Hebrew words with their meanings and a few references.
For more study on praise, there are other resources in the appendix.[10]

1. Hallal
Means to be clear, to praise, to shine, to boast, to rave, to celebrate, to be clamorously foolish. This is the kind of praise that is displayed at football matches, when the crowd gets very excited and boasts and yells as they cheer for their team.
All the words translated "praise" in Psalm 150are from Hallal.

2. Yada
Means to extend or throw out the hand, perhaps as in throwing a javelin, Also to lift hands in thanks. It is the opposite of "bemoaning or wringing of the hands." So it implies power, direction or thanksgiving. Like thrusting your fist in the air when something great happens.
Psalm 67:3. Let the peoples praise you, O God; let all the peoples praise you!

3. Toda

Means confession, praise and thanksgiving. It also implies an extension of the hands in adoration and thanksgiving. Occasionally translated praise, but also thanksgiving. A good illustration of this is when a small child extends their hands in adoration or thanks towards a parent and wants to be picked up.

Psalm 42:4 These things I remember, as I pour out my soul: how I would go with the throng and lead them in procession to the house of God with glad shouts and songs of praise, a multitude keeping festival.

4. Shabach

Means to shout, address in a loud tone, of command or triumph. This would be like people do sometimes with the word "YES!"

Psalm 145:4. One generation shall praise Your works to another, And shall declare Your mighty acts.

5. Barak

Means to kneel down in an act of blessing God, to salute or praise.

Notice that we usually associate kneeling with worship, but here it is translated praise.

Psalm 103:1 Praise the LORD, my soul; all my inmost being, praise his holy name. (NIV)

6. Zamar

Means to sing praise or make music. Zamar contains the idea of striking a musical instrument with the fingers.

Psalm 21:13 Be exalted, O LORD, in your strength! We will sing and praise your power.

7. Tehilla

Is derived from the word hallal, but means specifically to sing a hymn or song of praise. Again, it is boasting or celebrating, but expressed in song. Big bold and bragging. I am imagining a huge choir singing a majestic and uplifting song to the Lord.

Psalm 22:3 Yet you are holy, enthroned on the praises of Israel.

Thanksgiving

Thanksgiving is often mentioned in the Psalms and elsewhere in Scripture, which whilst not having its own word for "praise", can be a very important part of praise. Thanksgiving is also an action and a habit that shapes our thoughts and attitudes, so it is very powerful in maintaining our focus on God.

Consider the following Scripture:

I will offer to you the sacrifice of thanksgiving and call on the name of the LORD.

I will pay my vows to the LORD in the presence of all his people,
in the courts of the house of the LORD, in your midst, O Jerusalem.

Praise the LORD!
Psalm 116:16-17

This is a powerful statement because it is an exhortation to praise the Lord in the company of many people, and to offer God thanksgiving as a sacrifice.
It is very hard to thank God in the midst of difficult circumstances, and this is right where thanksgiving becomes a sacrifice. Nevertheless, if we will thank God even in the midst of difficulty, it changes our focus from our circumstances, to God and all his mercies and benefits, which really is a sacrifice.
Sometimes our thanksgiving comes with tears, sometimes our thanksgiving comes with jubilation.

We thank God for simple everyday things like our food, and we thank God in the midst of joy or adversity. From the simplest and most basic things, to the most perplexing and distressing things, it is always appropriate to thank the Lord.

Sing to the LORD with thanksgiving; make melody to our God on the lyre! (Psalm 147:7)

The Nature Of Praise as seen in the Psalms

We see from these definitions that praise encompasses a wide variety of expressions:
Shouting, Boasting loudly, Throwing up hands in power,

Reaching out hands in supplication or adoration, Shouting in a voice of triumph, Kneeling down to bless God, Making music to, for and about God, Singing songs to Him.

Praise could also be a combination of any or all of the above.

Notice that today we almost always associate praise with music and singing. However in reality, only two of the seven Hebrew words specifically mention music, Zamar and Tehilla.

So what I am suggesting is that our praise is limited and even impoverished, because we are missing a lot of the dimensions that Scripture portrays as praise. God is very specific about how He wants us to praise Him.

If we focus on one type of praise all the time (the sort of praise associated with music), we will become malnourished spiritually.

If you eat only one kind of food, your body will not be everything God meant it to be. So it is with praise. There are many different ways of praising the Lord and I believe we should explore them all.

This is a Scriptural admonition to everyone regardless of age, personality, culture, race or background.

People sometimes think that because God is so specific about things like praising Him, or about worshiping Him,

that He is being egocentric.
Nothing could be further from the truth. Everything God does, everything He wants us to do, is specifically designed for our benefit, not His.
When God says to praise him, it is not for his sake but ours. We change our focus by praising God.
It is almost impossible to be speaking or singing praise to God from your heart, and be thinking about other things. That is one way our thoughts can be renewed, and that is one way we can become transformed into His image (Romans 12:2). God does not need our praise, but for ourselves, we desperately need to be involved in praising him.

Praise is a very powerful aspect of our lives that is largely under-utilised in our everyday life, mostly relegated to an hour or so once a week, if that.
One of the best books ever written on the power of praise, is a book by Merlin Carothers, Prison To Praise. It was written back in 1970, but is still as fresh as if it was written yesterday. It is available online in several places. If you are interested in reading up on Praise, this book is highly recommended.

See more about praise in the appendix.[10]

The last six Psalms, 145 - 150, are so full of exhortations to praise that one can hardly read them without becoming overcome by His presence! Try reading them out LOUD, either by yourself or in a group.

Dancing

Even though dancing is not mentioned as a specific type of praise, Scripture resounds with many instances of encouragement to praise the Lord with dancing.
If you are at all inclined to dance, then rejoice and be joyful before Him in this way.
This is also liberating!
Just like everything else the Lord has given us, the enemy also tries to counterfeit it and produces a polluted version.
Let our focus always be Jesus In everything we do, and may He alone get all the glory.
Psalm 149:3 Let them praise his name with dancing, making melody to him with tambourine and lyre!
Psalm 150:4, 2 Sam 6:14, Jeremiah 31:13, Psalm 30:11.

And many more.

In Summary

We should now understand from this very brief glimpse at praise, that it is not the same as worship.
When I praise my wife, Alison, as I should and as I do, there are words of praise, gestures, even loud shouts, hugs and occasionally, songs.

I praise my wife, but I do not worship her.
Worship is only directed to God.
We should praise God and we should also worship Him.
But worship is not the same thing as praise.

Here is a brief summary of the characteristics of praise and the characteristics of worship that we find in the Old Testament

Praise	Worship
Shouting, Boasting,	Bowing or prostrating oneself
Throwing hands, Reaching hands	Sacrifice - of a person's possessions
Shouting in triumph	Offering - Money or time
Kneeling	Prayer - usually by a priest
Making music with instruments	Declaration - Saying what God says
Singing	

If worship is so important, and is a major theme in the Bible, we should see it in many places in the New Testament, right?

Right.

And that is the topic of our next Chapter.

5. Worship and the New Testament

Here's a review of what we have learned so far.

We have seen that because the Father is seeking people to worship Him, then that must be very important. So we need to understand exactly what worship is, in order to be the ones found by the Father.

We discovered that the first mention of worship in Genesis when Abraham offered up Isaac is very significant, because this is the beginning of a major theme in Scripture.

Then we saw from some Old Testament examples, that worship actually has very little emphasis on music.

Next we examined the Psalms to see the exact nature of praise, and saw that even though worship is mentioned in the Psalms (11 times) , praise is mentioned many more. (over 120 times)

Praise is not the same as worship, and it is a major emphasis in the Psalms.

In this Chapter, we will explore the New Testament to see how worship is worked out in Jesus' life, and the life and teaching of the first disciples.

Before we can get too involved in analysing the life of Jesus and the disciples regarding worship, I would like to present this illustration of the major difference between the Old Testament and the New Testament.
Understanding the differences between the Old and New Testaments, is fundamental to how we interpret Scripture, and we will look at the critical importance of that in detail later. But for now, let's look at just one major difference.

Once before we came to Malaysia, we were at a travel agency in Australia. In the racks of brochures, were advertising pamphlets showing the marvellous islands and tropical wonders available in Malaysia. It all looked like a wonderful place to visit.
After we got to Malaysia, and on one weekend actually went snorkelling off a small town called Semporna, we experienced for ourselves what the travel brochures meant. We could see everything in 3-D. We could feel the beach, the boat, the warmth of the tropical water, we could smell the food, the fishing boats and the tropical humidity, we could hear the sounds of the local waters, vendors and

language.
The brochure was the picture pointing to the real place, but was not the experience.

The Old Testament is a bit like that travel brochure. It is pointing to the New Testament.
The brochure has pictures that are real and information that is correct, but the experience can only be described by being there, not simply understood from the descriptions in the brochure.

So it is with the Old Testament. It contains information, pictures, illustrations and situations that point to the New Testament. It points to the reality of life in the New Covenant. Specifically, life in Jesus and direct open access to the Father.
Here is what Jesus said to the Scribes and Pharisees of the day:

You search the Scriptures because you think that in them you have eternal life; and it is they that bear witness about me, yet you refuse to come to me that you may have life. (John 5:39-40)

The New Testament is the destination that the Old Testament is describing, just like the travel brochure describes the destination. Everything in the Old Testament points to Jesus. The New Testament is the fulfilment of God's plan, the endpoint and culmination of history. It is the destination of the journey.

But the analogy is too simplistic because the Bible is vastly more complex than that. Everything in the Old Testament points to the New Testament. But much of the New Testament can only be understood fully, by reference to and by knowing the Old Testament.
Jesus, Paul, Peter, John and Jude all continually referred to and quoted the Old Testament.

So we can be sure that study of the Old Testament is absolutely necessary.

St Augustine wrote a saying, which is widely quoted:
"The Old Testament is the New Testament concealed, and the New Testament is the Old Testament revealed."

St. Augustine.[11]

We call the pictures, illustrations and analogies in the Old Testament, types and shadows. They are the picture pointing to the real thing.
There are many such types, and we see Jesus illustrated many times in the Old Testament.

For example, Isaac was a type of Jesus. He willingly submitted to being sacrificed by his father even though the Lord at the last moment spared him. But Jesus was the reality of the type. The Father really did sacrifice his Son on the cross as a perfect, finished and once-for-all offering. To add to the intensity of this image, the hill that Abraham went to with Isaac, was possibly the same hill on which Jesus was crucified.[12]

Until Jesus came, the only experience that Israel had of God, was the Old Testament.
So when Jesus started preaching new things, they were hard to accept. His teaching was radically different from anything they had heard before. But Jesus' teaching was noticeably different from that of the Scribes and Pharisees. His teaching had authority that was widely recognised. (Mark 1:21-22)

The Radical Shift To Father

Jesus said something radical things to the the woman at the well in Samaria (John 4:4-26).
He said it was no longer important where people worship God, but that worship would be from the heart. He also referred to God as the Father, and taught his disciples to refer to God as "our" Father.
In the Old Testament, God is occasionally referred to as the Father of Israel in a general sense, but individuals did not know God personally in this way.
Jesus had a unique relationship with the Father, and He made a way for us to share in that same relationship. This was not the relationship with God that people in the Old Testament had.
Our relationship with God, the Creator and Ruler of the Universe, is now characterised by a unique word: "Father".

Nobody in the Old Testament, ever called God their "father".
Not the prophets, not the priests, not the kings,
Not Abraham, Moses or David,
Not even Adam.

Here is what Jesus said:

"But the hour is coming, and is now here, when the true worshipers will worship the Fatherin spirit and truth, for the Fatheris seeking such people to worship him." (John 4:23)

Jesus was starting to show that there was a fundamental and life-changing shift going to begin in their understanding of worship. It began with a shift in their understanding of their relationship with God, and it begins there for us too.

In the "sermon on the mount" as it is called in Matthew Chapters 5 and 6, we see Jesus explaining people's heart motives. Even thinking about something was the same as actually doing it.

"You have heard that it was said, 'You shall not commit adultery.' But I say to you that everyone who looks at a woman with lustful intent has already committed adultery with her in his heart. (Matt 5:27-28)

It is the heart motive that Jesus was exposing. Jesus also addresses anger in the same way:

"You have heard that it was said to the people long ago, 'You shall not murder, and anyone who murders will be subject to judgment.' But I tell you that anyone who is angry with a brother or sister will be subject to judgment. Again, anyone who says to a brother or sister, 'Raca,' is answerable to the court. And anyone who says, 'You fool!' will be in danger of the fire of hell.(Matt 5:22)

Jesus was pointing out that the reason for people's behaviour, is the attitude of their heart.

This is because the New Covenant is internal to a person's nature, whilst the Old Covenant was external. The Old was concerned with a person's behaviour, whilst the New deals with a person's motives. This is why the Old Testament prophesies pointed to the laws being written on our hearts and not on tablets of stone anymore. Jeremiah in the Old Testament prophesied of the New Covenant:

"Behold, the days are coming, declares the LORD, when I will make a new covenant with the house of Israel and the house of Judah, not like the covenant that I made with their fathers on the day when I took them by the hand to bring them out of the land of Egypt, my covenant that they broke, though I was their husband, declares the LORD.

For this is the covenant that I will make with the house of Israel after those days, declares the LORD: I will put my law within them, and

I will write it on their hearts. And I will be their God, and they shall be my people.
And no longer shall each one teach his neighbour and each his brother, saying, 'Know the LORD,' for they shall all know me, from the least of them to the greatest, declares the LORD. For I will forgive their iniquity, and I will remember their sin no more."
(Jeremiah 31:31-34, Hebrews 8:8-12)

God knows that our heart is wicked and all the issues of life flow from there. He knew that we needed a heart transplant and He had prepared a way to make that happen. Jeremiah 17:9 explains that the root of our idol worship and our turning away from God, is caused by our heart.
But then He states later in Jeremiah that God will write His laws on our hearts. This is what happens when we are born again.

So, what does this have to do with worship?

Everything.

We are told in Hebrews 11:6 that without faith it is impossible to please God.
We also know that the Father is seeking those who will worship Him.
Therefore it is evident that worshipers must be those who please Him.

So faith must be integral with our worship. Worship is actually an expression of our faith.

One of the foundational things about being a worshiper, is our relationship to the Father.

Let's see how Jesus introduces this in Matthew's Gospel.

Matthew Chapter 6 (and also Luke Chapter 11) records Jesus' response to a request made by His disciples, that He would teach them how to pray.
Jesus responds this way in Matt 6:9, *'Pray then like this: Our Father in Heaven, hallowed be your name."*
We are so familiar with this Scripture, that the extreme, radical nature of such a statement from Jesus is often lost on us.

Jesus told His disciples to address God as their Father; In fact, "our" Father.

That means they were His sons - well not quite yet, but after He shed His blood and then rose from the grave and they accepted His incredible gift of life - then they were His sons.
Next He told them to declare that the name of the Father was holy. "Hallowed" means, holy, blameless, sacred, and it is so very, very special and precious.

So now, God is their Father. This was a radical statement in the traditional thinking of the Pharisees, and they saw this as blasphemy. It is no surprise that later, Saul vigorously persecuted this new sect of disciples. It is also one of the reasons why the Pharisees sought to kill Jesus.

We are looking at a radical and complete relationship shift here, from the Old Testament to the New Testament.

God has not changed, but our relationship to Him has.
The shift is from one of seeing and acknowledging God from a distance, to one of fellowship with God as a Father. Jesus called this change "The Kingdom Of God". To be in God's Kingdom, you must be born again. When we are in the Kingdom, we have a King and His name is Jesus. That also means we are His subjects.
This "father relationship" is one of the most important and intimate in life, defining much about us. It is no surprise that the enemy of our souls, the devil, is supremely focused on polluting or destroying one of the primary relationships of life. Satan does not want you to worship God.

Let us pause here for a moment, because I know that none of us have had perfect fathers, and so our perception of the Father relationship has been polluted.
This is a primary enemy focus - polluting the relationship with the father.
His intention is to "steal, kill and destroy" as we see in John 10:10.

HOWEVER…
Jesus said: "but I came that you might have life and have it abundantly". (John 10:10)
This is the most incredible and amazing thing about the Gospel.
Jesus has come to set us free from all the damage, pollution, hurts and scars and everything that the enemy has been using to attempt to destroy us. Jesus came to replace our hearts.

God did not change from the Old Testament to the New Testament. But our hearts can and so can our relationship with the Father. We cannot change our heart, but God does.
The Gospel introduces us to the most powerful relationship in the universe, that we can become God's sons and daughters, and He is our Father.

What we are starting to see, is that Jesus is bringing us into the reality of the picture we glimpsed in the Old Testament. The Old Testament picture of worship that we saw in type, can become the pattern for the way we live.
To be a worshiper, we need to worship the Father in spirit and truth, and God is looking for those people.

Worshipers are those whose relationship with the Father is healed, intact and flourishing. The Father is the primary focus of worship, and this focus is only achievable as we accept the provisions of new life - being born again as Jesus provided in the New Covenant. We see in the Old Covenant the picture, the type, the shadow of the real worship that was to come. In the Old Testament, they had to worship in types and shadows.

As we continue to journey through the New Testament exploring worship, we will see that Jesus models for us the real nature of true worship.

The Occasion Of The Expensive Perfume

Here is a powerful occasion of worship, even though that word is not specifically used to describe the incident. The incident is recorded in all of the four Gospels, where a woman poured a jar of really expensive perfume on Jesus.

There are actually two separate occasions of this, one involving a person called Mary and the other a "sinful woman", but they were not the same person.

This can be a little confusing at first, because on a casual reading it would be easy to think all the Gospel accounts were referring to the same event.

But this is not so, and it is necessary to understand the difference. This is important because otherwise, strange and unwarranted ideas can be deduced, which lead in turn to false conclusions.

Here are the accounts, in the order in which they occur in the four Gospels.

Matthew 26:6-13

While Jesus was in Bethany in the home of Simon the Leper, a woman came to him with an alabaster jar of very expensive perfume, which she poured on his head as he was reclining at the table. When the disciples saw this, they were indignant. "Why this waste?" they asked. "This perfume could have been sold at a high price and the money given to the poor." Aware of this, Jesus said to them, "Why are you bothering this woman? She has done a beautiful thing to me. The poor you will always have with you, but you will not always have me. When she poured this perfume on my body, she did it to prepare me for burial. Truly I tell you, wherever this gospel is preached throughout the world, what she has done will also be told, in memory of her.

Mark 14:3-9

While he was in Bethany, reclining at the table in the home of Simon the Leper, a woman came with an alabaster jar of very expensive perfume, made of pure nard. She broke the jar and poured the perfume on his head. Some of those present were saying indignantly to one another, "Why this waste of perfume? It could have been sold for more than a year's wages and the money given to the poor." And they rebuked her harshly. "Leave her alone," said Jesus. "Why are you bothering her? She has done a beautiful thing to me. The poor you will always have with you, and you can help them any time you want. But you will not always have me. She did what she could. She poured perfume on my body beforehand to prepare for my burial. Truly I tell you, wherever the gospel is preached throughout the world, what she has done will also be told, in memory of her."

Luke 7:36-39

When one of the Pharisees invited Jesus to have dinner with him, he went to the Pharisee's house and reclined at the table. A woman in that town who lived a sinful life learned that Jesus was eating at the Pharisee's house, so she came there with an alabaster jar of perfume. As she stood behind him at his feet weeping, she began to wet his feet with her tears. Then she wiped them with her hair, kissed them and poured perfume on them. When the Pharisee who had invited him saw this, he said to himself, "If this man were a prophet, he would know who is touching him and what kind of woman she is—that she is a sinner."

John 12:1-8

Six days before the Passover, Jesus came to Bethany, where Lazarus lived, whom Jesus had raised from the dead. Here a dinner was given in Jesus' honor. Martha served, while Lazarus was among those reclining at the table with him. Then Mary took about a pint of pure nard, an expensive perfume; she poured it on Jesus' feet and wiped his feet with her hair. And the house was filled with the fragrance of the perfume. But one of his disciples, Judas Iscariot, who was later to betray him, objected, "Why wasn't this perfume sold and the money given to the poor? It was worth a year's wages." He did not say this because he cared about the poor but because he was a thief; as keeper of the money bag, he used to help himself to what was put into it. "Leave her alone," Jesus replied. "It was intended that she should save this perfume for the day of my burial. You will always have the poor among you, but you will not always have me."

We see immediately that the accounts of Matthew and Mark are so similar that it would not be logical for them to be different occasions.

John's account of this event is also very similar to Matthew and Mark's, with a couple of small but significant details.

Luke's account on the other hand is so different from the others, that it cannot be considered to be the same occasion.

Here is a comparison summary of the four accounts.

	Matthew	Mark	John	Luke
Location	Bethany	Bethany	Bethany	Not stated but probably Capernaum
Place	Simon the Leper's house	Simon the Leper's house	Not stated but assumed to be Simon the leper's house	Simon the Pharisee's house *
When	Not long before the crucifixion - "preparation for burial"	Not long before the crucifixion - "preparation for burial"	Six days before the Passover	Not accurately known, but because John the Baptist was still alive, probably two years or so earlier.
Audience	Disciples, Simon and the woman - more?	Disciples, Simon and the woman - more?	Disciples, Lazarus, Martha, and Mary - more?	The Pharisee, the woman and guests of the Pharisee. No mention of the disciples
Spice	Expensive perfume in an Alabaster jar	Nard, an expensive perfume in an alabaster jar	Nard, an expensive perfume worth a year's wages	An Alabaster jar of perfume
Person	An unnamed woman poured it on Jesus' head	An unnamed woman poured it on Jesus' head	Mary, the sister of Lazarus and Martha, poured it on Jesus' feet	A woman of the town. Possibly a prostitute because the Pharisee objected to her presence. She poured it on Jesus' feet
People's Response	Wasteful - the perfume could have been sold	Wasteful - the perfume could have been sold	Wasteful - it could have been sold	If Jesus was a prophet, he would know who this woman was
Jesus' Response	She has done this for my burial	She has done this for my burial	She has done has done this for my burial	Jesus rebuked the Pharisee and told the parable of the moneylender who forgave large and small debts
Common phrases	...for my burial... ...do not bother her she has done a beautiful thing... ...The poor you always have with you... ...this will be told in memory of her...	...for my burial... ...do not bother her she has done a beautiful thing... ...The poor you always have with you... ...this will be told in memory of her...	...for my burial... ...the poor you will always have with you...	No phrases in common with Matthew Mark or John.
Common	Jesus was anointed with very expensive perfume by a woman.			

* Simon the Pharisee is a different person from Simon the Leper. A leper would never have been allowed to be a

Pharisee, and if he contracted leprosy whilst he was a Pharisee, he would have been permanently excluded from their ranks

This summary is simply to help us understand these incidents more fully.

There are other things which can be studied from this anointing of Jesus, but I want to focus particularly on the one thing which is common to all the accounts.
And this I believe, is the main reason why the incident is included in Scripture.

Jesus was anointed with expensive perfume by a woman.

Where did a women get this kind of perfume, seeing that women were not wage earners in that time? The answer lies in understanding that although in their culture, a woman had very few personal possessions of her own, she did have her own dowry which was bestowed on her as a young girl by her father.
The precious anointing perfume was meant to be saved and used first on their wedding night. It was an act of using everything she had for her husband, declaring that he was now her most treasured possession.[13]

This simple gesture of the woman is a massive act of worship, and its significance can hardly be overlooked.
She was pouring out everything she owned on Jesus in one lavish and extravagant act of love.
This was her substance, her future, her hopes and dreams. By anointing Jesus in this way, she was quite possibly forfeiting her dowry and her chance of marriage. In the culture of the time, being unmarried was a stigma and a disgrace.

In a prophetic way which they could not have understood at the time, they were declaring symbolically that Jesus was their husband, that they were the Bride Of Christ.
In hindsight we can see the symbolism, because now in a very real way, we also are being prepared as His Bride.

We can not pour out anything on Jesus in a physical way anymore, but we have something far more precious under the New Covenant which we can pour out, we have our redeemed lives.

When we are baptised, we die to our old life and rise to new life in Jesus. Paul puts it this way in Romans Chapter 12.

I appeal to you therefore, brothers, by the mercies of God, to present your bodies as a living sacrifice, holy and acceptable to God, which is your spiritual worship. (Romans 12:1)

Notice how Paul says that by presenting our bodies as a living sacrifice, we are engaging in worship.
God knows that by offering ourselves this way, we are voluntarily becoming completely His, to use as His possession. This is the place of complete and permanent surrender of our will, to the Father's will.
In the typology of the Old Covenant, the sacrifice was completely consumed on the altar. Also, as it is obvious, the offering never got down from the altar. The offering became a fragrance to God that He accepted and was pleased with.
Now we begin to see why the Father is seeking worshipers - those who will completely surrender their will to His.

Permanently.

This is most precious.

Worship is not something God desires because He is egocentric, nor does he actually need anything from us - He is innately sufficient and complete. We have nothing to offer Him.

However,
He knows that if we worship anything but Him, we will be

unfulfilled.
He knows that as we lose our lives for His sake, we will find them.
He knows that as we discover the true nature of worship, we will become the ones that He is seeking.

Everything the Father does is for our benefit, not His.

Before we move on from this event, there is something else I want to highlight from these passages.

In both Matthew's and Mark's account of this event, Jesus says, *"wherever the Gospel is preached through the world, what she has done will be told in memory of her".*This extravagant act of worship needs to be told and re-told.

Told "wherever the Gospel is preached throughout the world".

These are Jesus' words, so I do believe we should be including the event of The Expensive Oil, in our preaching of the Gospel.

We should be including the example of worship that Mary illustrated, as part of our Gospel message.

The complete self-sacrifice that is worship, needs to be clearly spelled out as we come to Jesus.

This is because worship is the essence of our being. We are madeto worship, we willworship because we are designedto worship. The enemy's biggest thrust is to get us to worship anything except God. Before we were saved, we were by default, worshiping in the enemy's kingdom.

God is seeking those who will worship Him.

The problem is, that only the worship of God can truly satisfy us.
Everything else is hollow, empty and polluted. And the enemy has made sure that our understanding of real worship is clouded, obscure and unfocused.
When we present the Gospel, we do not usually spell out the purity and simplicity of sacrificing everything we have and are, as the main component of worship.

Mary had sacrificed everything she was, everything she had, everything she hoped to be, on Jesus.
Then He died.

What must have been going through Mary's heart and mind when Jesus died? She had poured out her substance, her living, her future on Jesus. But now He was dead and probably in her own mind, so was she.
But that is what the Father is seeking.

The New Testament often talks about taking up our cross daily, dying to self, crucifying the flesh, living the life that Jesus has called us to live in His strength, not in our own strength.[14]

Mary's joy would have been so extreme when she knew that Jesus had risen and was alive.

Her sacrifice, her life, was not wasted or in vain, in fact, it was fulfilled.

Now that we have seen an example of real worship expressed in the life of a couple of disciples, let's move on to the role of music and worship in the New Testament.

6. Worship and Music

We saw in chapter 5 that our relationship to the Father is a foundational aspect of the way we express our worship. This was a radical and new concept to Jesus' disciples, which involved a heart transplant.

We saw how two women demonstrated their sacrifice of worship by pouring out their lives on Jesus, and now we are starting to see that by offering ourselves as a living sacrifice, we are worshiping the Father.

But normally when we think of "worship", we automatically assume that there is music involved. This is because the Christian Music Marketing Machine has promoted the 'Praise and Worship" genre as being the normal description for worship. Indeed, that is most people's experience.

However as we have already seen in Scripture, music is not necessarily a part of worship at all.
Not according to the descriptions of worship in the Old or the New Testaments.

The Bible must be our basis and foundation for what we do when we worship God.
The Father is seeking those who will worship Him in spirit and in truth, so our understanding of worship must be that which God is seeking. Nothing else.

There is some reference to the association of music and worship in the Old Testament, but very little in the New Testament.

It was mystifying to me as a musician, to read through the New Testament and find that there is surprisingly little reference to music or musicians. Almost nothing.
The New Testament is mostly quiet about the role of music in our worship. Since this is so, there must be much more to worship than music and singing.

Here is a list of the places "music and worship" are mentioned together in the New Testament.

1. ______________

There isa place where music is mentioned in a parable told by Jesus of the Prodigal son, where the elder brother came in from the field and heard the party (dancing and music) Luke 15:25. But apart from that, almost nothing. Seriously.

Did Jesus talk about music and singing? Well, not too much as we already have seen.

But there is one reference that gives us a clue. Luke records a time when Jesus jumped for joy.
Yes, like throwing high fives and dancing!
It is in Luke Chapter 10. When the disciples came back after being sent out by two, to cast out demons and heal the sick.

Jesus got their report and here's what He did:

In that same hour he rejoiced in the Holy Spirit and said, "I thank you, Father, Lord of heaven and earth, that you have hidden these things from the wise and understanding and revealed them to little children; yes, Father, for such was your gracious will. (Luke 10:21)

The Greek word[15]which we translate into the word "rejoiced" means "exult, rejoice exceedingly, leap for joy". Sounds a bit like some of the Hebrew praise words we looked at in Chapter 4.
Jesus is not lacking in joy or the expression of it.

The night before Jesus was crucified, after they had finished their Passover meal, they sang a hymn and went out to the garden. This was possibly Psalm 118. According to Jewish Passover tradition, Psalms 113 to 118 were sung during the Passover celebration.[16]

And when they had sung a hymn, they went out to the Mount of Olives. (Matt 26:30)
(Mar 14:27–31; Luk 22:31–34; Jhn 13:36–38)

Even though there are no references to music in the New Testament, there area very few references to singing, which is also music. But the circumstances under which the singing was mentioned, were definitely less than ideal. Not your typical church setting.
For instance in Acts, where Paul and Silas were in prison for preaching the Gospel, they were praying and singing hymns.

About midnight Paul and Silas were praying and singing hymns to God, and the prisoners were listening to them, and suddenly there was a great earthquake so that the foundations of the prison were shaken. (Acts 16:25-26)

We would love to see foundations shaken when we sing! But it is not about the song, it is about the moving of the Holy Spirit.

In his letters to the Ephesians and to the Colossians, Paul mentions three different musical terms: psalms, hymns and spiritual songs. I believe that the reason Paul uses different words here - although the full meaning in Greek is not that precise because they overlap a lot[17]- is that Paul is referring to different *kinds* of songs. Paul is encouraging them to build one another up and also to bring teaching and correction by means of song.

Psalms, Hymns and Spiritual Songs could be described this way:

Psalms are music or songs used in Scripture - from the Psalms mostly;
Hymns are the traditional set pieces of music used by the Church from former years;
Spiritual songs are those the Spirit births in your heart, either pre-written or spontaneous.

Or put in another way:

Psalms - Scripture set to music
Hymns - Testimony of the old saints
Spiritual Songs - From the Saints of today

And yet another way:

Psalms - our foundation
Hymns - our past testimony
Spiritual Songs - our present testimony

But whichever way you describe Psalms, Hymns and Spiritual Songs, singing is important to Paul and therefore we should think so too. He wants us to use songs to teach, edify and build one another up.

...addressing one another in psalms and hymns and spiritual songs, singing and making melody to the Lord with your heart, (Ephesians 5:19)

Let the word of Christ dwell in you richly, teaching and admonishing one another in all wisdom, singing psalms and hymns and spiritual songs, with thankfulness in your hearts to God.
Colossians 3:16)

Also in first Corinthians we find Paul mentioning hymns:

What then, brothers? When you come together, each one has a hymn, a lesson, a revelation, a tongue, or an interpretation. Let all things be done for building up. (1 Cor 14:26)

What am I to do? I will pray with my spirit, but I will pray with my mind also; I will sing praise with my spirit, but I will sing with my mind also. (1 Cor 14:15)

In context in Corinthians (and remember that a text without a context is a con), Paul is giving instructions

about their meetings because they had become unruly.
This is not Paul's instruction about music, and it is not instruction about worship, and it is not teaching about praise.
Paul is instructing them on how to build one another up. His intent is not to bring a teaching about music and praise.

In these passages, Ephesians, Colossians and Corinthians, Paul's main concern is that they are edifying one another.

It is important to see that the association we have made between music and worshipis not part of the New Covenant.

Even in Revelation when the angel is showing John what is happening in Heaven, there is surprisingly, almost no music.
There is however, a song that a 144,000 people sang in front of the throne, but no-one else was allowed to learn it. It is reserved for 144,000 Jewish virgin men. (Rev 14:2-3)

Make no mistake though, Heaven is a very LOUD place! Worship and praise in Heaven are thunderously loud and unceasing, but it is spoken, not sung.
Except for a half hour in heaven that is silent. (Revelation 8:1)
Angels do not sing, not anywhere in Scripture. They don't

do that. Angels did not sing when Jesus was born[18]and they do not sing in Heaven.

Often, people say they want to learn to play an instrument because they want to be able to worship the Lord. That is a mistaken concept. Both Old and New Testaments place no priority on music as an essential part of worship.

But while there is a deafening silence in the New Testament on the use of music, there is an enormous amount said about worship.

Let's look briefly at some more examples of worship in the New Testament. They seem to be hidden, but I do believe that is because our paradigm filters out the important things, because our "worship filter" has been so preconditioned.

We have confused Worship with Praise, and so do not understand the true nature of worship.

We think that what we are doing in church is worship, when most of the time it actually is not. This is a major enemy strategy, to confuse our understanding of worship.

Worship is a profoundly important major theme in Scripture, because the Father is seeking those who will worship Him.

(John 4:23)
But worship has very little to do with music, in fact in the New Testament, nothing at all!

In the next chapter we will have a look at the New Testament as our comprehensive worship manual.

7. Worship and Offering Ourselves

Oh, the depth of the riches and wisdom and knowledge of God! How unsearchable are his judgments and how inscrutable his ways! "For who has known the mind of the Lord, or who has been his counselor?" "Or who has given a gift to him that he might be repaid?" For from him and through him and to him are all things. To him be glory forever. Amen.
I appeal to you therefore, brothers, by the mercies of God, to present your bodies as a living sacrifice, holy and acceptable to God, which is your spiritual worship.
(Romans 11:33-12:1)

Many times we just read a verse or two as if they are "stand alone" statements that speak for themselves. Very occasionally that is true, but most of the time we need to see verses in their setting, to understand what the Lord is really saying to us through this Scripture.

If I was away from my wife for work and I wrote her a letter, I would not index the letter with paragraph and sentence numbers. If I did and she wrote back in her reply, "but you said in paragraph 3 line 25…" , that would be almost absurd. No, we do not communicate in an analytically mechanical way like that. To do so, would imply almost zero understanding of the person and the relationship. It could also lead to gross misunderstanding of what a person is really saying.

When I write Alison a letter, she knows me, she knows why I am writing and I know who she is and where she is and how she thinks.

So it is with the letters in the New Testament, and in fact in all the books we have in the Bible. They are a communication to us from our Father, and we limit our understanding by clinically dissecting the books with the numbering system we invented.[19]

When I used to teach Biology, we would occasionally dissect a rabbit in class. They could be ordered from a laboratory supplies company, and came injected with formalin (a preservative) and wrapped in sterile plastic bags.

I was careful during the dissection, to display and explain the organs and their functions, and the students gained some understanding of the structure and function of the internal organs of a rabbit. But the students did not know rabbits, just the sum of their parts.

However, we lived on a farm for about thirteen years, and observed rabbits in their natural habitat. We saw them living, eating, reproducing, socialising, and dying. We saw them in their totality of their life cycle. Some people even keep rabbits as pets.

This produces more understanding of rabbits than clinically dissecting them ever could.

Just like my students did not really know rabbits even though they knew their parts, the numbering system in our Bibles is an artificial addition to the Word of God which man has invented. It allows us to dissect the Word of God clinically and precisely, but then it tends to become sterile and devoid of life.

Of course the Chapter and verse numbers are useful for study, reference and memorising. This book uses the numbering system that way too. But for complete understanding, we need to ignore the numbers when we read Scripture. This makes the context clear.

A text without a context is a con.

With everything we read in the Bible, we should know who the person is who is writing this letter, and what they were like. We should know why the letter or book was written, what was its cultural and sociological context, and to whom was it written. This knowledge will greatly enhance our depth of understanding of Scripture.

An invaluable resource in this regard is David Pawson's, Unlocking The Bible.Pawson goes through each book in the Bible in historical and sociological context, and gives definitive and well researched information on all these issues.[20]

We also need to understand when we read Scripture, that the Jews knew their Scriptures well. (the Old Testament). They all were immersed in the Scriptures from an early age, and knew them by heart. You could not live as a Jew and not be familiar with the Scriptures.

When we are very familiar with documents or literature, a word or a small phrase is sufficient to remind us of the whole passage and context. And so it was with the Jews. When Jesus, and the New Testament writers spoke or wrote to their audience and referred to Scripture (which was always Old Testament), their listeners would automatically have known the context to which they were referring.

Many phrases in our own everyday communication work this way. We can say a word, or a phrase that has a fuller meaning.
Things like, "many hands"… or "a bird in the hand"… or "a stitch in time"…

Just like that, when Jesus, or any of the New Testament writers quote Scripture, they were quoting it to an audiences which were themselves, very familiar with the passages. Therefore just a word or a phrase was enough to remind them of the whole story or passage. The New Testament writers did not need to rehearse large portions of Scripture to their listeners or readers in order for them to understand. The Scriptures were already familiar to them.

So when Paul begins Romans Chapter 12 with "therefore", his readers would have easily recognised why that should be so, and they would not have paused at a "chapter break".

But it is not necessarily that way with us. We live in a different culture and setting, and are (mostly) not as familiar with the Scriptures as Paul's audience was.
This is why I have also included the last few verses of Romans 11 with Romans 12 in the above quote.

Because of God's incredible wisdom, knowledge, judgements and ways, we should as a response of worship, offer Him the only thing we actually have which is of any value.
Ourselves.
Our Redeemed Selves.

The price Jesus paid to redeem us was extreme, which is why our redeemed life is worth anything at all. It also cost the Father an unfathomable amount.
The Father and The Son, paid an incomprehensible price for our redemption.
Now that we are redeemed, we have an inestimable worth to Him. Before that, we were unworthy and of no value.

Paul calls this a "living sacrifice", holy, acceptable to God, which is true worship.

The New International Version puts it this way:

Therefore, I urge you, brothers and sisters, in view of God's mercy, to offer your bodies as a living sacrifice, holy and pleasing to God—this is your true and proper worship. (Rom 12:1 NIV)

Being or becoming a "living sacrifice", touches every area of our lives.
Sacrifice involves giving up things:
Our will
Our "rights"
Our possessions
Our time
Our ambitions
Our achievements
Our talents
Our pride
Our failures
Everything.

God wants us to know that if we are willing to do that, He will use everything to the good for His glory and His Kingdom. "*And we know that for those who love God all things work together for good, for those who are called according to his purpose.*"
(Romans 8:28)

Abraham offered Isaac to God in the way God wanted him to.
For Abraham, Isaac represented the fulfilment of everything God had ever promised him. Abraham's will, achievements, ambitions, hopes and dreams, were all dependent on Isaac. And God asked Abraham to give them all up.
It was a test. God wanted Abraham to demonstrate to himself and to God, that there was no other priority in his life higher than God. And Abraham did that without reservation, so God proceeded with the plan. God already knew what Abraham would do, but this test was mostly for Abraham's benefit.

However it was not just Abraham who benefited from this test, since we also are beneficiaries of his obedience. We see in Abraham's life, an example of true worship which involved obedience to the Father and belief in what God had promised. And so it was counted to him as righteousness, even before Jesus died.
(See Romans 4 and Hebrews 11)

The women who poured out their living on Jesus, did the same thing as Abraham did.

We cannot worship the Father without sacrifice.

Worship

God asks us to make the offering of our living bodies. Holy bodies.

Now we are getting into the reality of life in Jesus. This is our real worship.

This involves how we use our eyes, how we use our hands, the things we listen to, the way we talk, the things we eat, the places our feet take us and the way we relate to other people.

This is why so much of the New Testament is about how we live, how we love, how we give and even how we talk. James talks very strongly about how we use our tongues.

With it we bless our Lord and Father, and with it we curse people who are made in the likeness of God. From the same mouth come blessing and cursing. My brothers, these things ought not to be so. (James 3:9-10)

If our bodies are indeed offered up to God as a living sacrifice, then our tongue is a part of that sacrifice. This is full-time worship.

Do blessing and cursing both come from our mouths? This should not be so. If cursing (the opposite of blessing) comes out of our mouths, we are not worshiping God as we should. Cursing is not just saying cuss words. Cursing is the opposite of blessing.

But God's big weapon to destroy and repair this situation, is repentance. Telling Him you know you have done wrong and then doing the opposite.

Repentance is not a feeling, it is an action. This also is part of our worship.
In Ephesians 4:17-32, Paul details exactly how this life in Jesus plays out in everyday experience. Paul describes repentance without actually using that word, but shows us the actions that go with repentance. They are opposites.

The opposite of lying is telling the truth (V25)
The opposite of anger is not giving the devil an opportunity (V26,27)
The opposite of stealing is giving (V28)
The opposite of cursing is blessing (V29)
The opposite of bitterness, wrath, anger, clamour and slander is
kindness, tenderheartedness and forgiveness (V31,32)
And as we act that way, we do not grieve the Holy Spirit. (V30)

You can tell that a liar has repented, when he starts telling the truth.

Not when he stops lying.
You can tell if a thief has repented when he starts giving.

Not when he stops stealing.
You can tell if a person has repented of cursing when he starts blessing.

Not when he stops cursing.
That is Paul's point. Real repentance is doing the opposite.

You don't repent by just stopping doing negative things. That just eliminates the negatives and gets you to zero. Repentance is complete when you start doing the opposite. Think of a thermometer. If you just eliminate the negatives, you are only at zero and still cold. God wants us to live in the heat. A life full of warmth and vibrance powered by the Holy Spirit, warming and giving life to those we touch.

Repentance is one of God's powerful tools for shaping our character, and filling us with the warmth and vibrance others so desperately need.

Repent therefore, and turn back, that your sins may be blotted out, that times of refreshing may come from the presence of the Lord, and that he may send the Christ appointed for you, Jesus… (Acts 3:19-20)

Repentance brings refreshing, cancellation of sins, changes in our character, a renewed presence of Jesus and so much

more.
God urges us to be holy as He is holy. That means set apart, consecrated to Him, dedicated for His use only. This is a life of worship.

What we are starting to see is that the Father is looking for those who will voluntarily and freely offer their lives to Him as a sacrifice, every moment of every day, which is a major theme in the New Testament.

However, the perplexing bit is that we do not see "worship" embraced as a topic in the New Testament.
We can find repentance as a topic and we can find baptism as a topic. We know about Jesus' return, judgement, forgiveness and other topics, but not specifically the topic of worship.
This is simply because we have not understood that worship is about the way we live.
If we were to look up the topic of "the way we live", we do not find that neatly spelt out, but it is everywhere in the New Testament, specifically Acts and all the letters.
And Jesus taught on this too.
Here are some of the things we do find in Scripture about how to live.

(This list is nowhere near complete, and there are many other references you can find to each one)

If you lose your life you will find it (Matt 10:39)
Crucify the flesh (Gal 5:24)
Embrace suffering and count it as joy (James 1:2)
Endure to the end (Matt 24:13)
Rejoice always (1 Thess 5:16)
Love your enemies (Luke 6:27)
Serve your brothers and sisters (Gal 5:13)

This list is simply part of everything that Jesus wants us to do, and everything Peter, Paul, James, John and Jude encourage us to do. These are all about the way we should live as Disciples of Jesus, and this is our worship.

A life lived with a focus on pleasing God, is a life lived in worship to Him.
This is why Jesus can tell us that it is not important where we worship, but how we worship. It is all about being a living sacrifice. No wonder the Father is seeking these kinds of people. How we live is how we worship. This is why worship cannot be contained in a song and why worship in the New Testament is not specifically associated with music or songs.

When the song is over, have we stopped worshiping? This can not be so, for it is not what the Father is seeking.
The Father's desire and His search for worshipers is not that frivolous.

But the hour is coming, and is now here, when the true worshipers will worship the Father in spirit and truth, for the Father is seeking such people to worship him. (John 4:23)

Jesus calls us to become His disciples.
He calls us to forgive as we have been forgiven (Matt 6:14)
He calls us to love others as He has loved us (John 13:34)
He calls us to heal the sick, cleanse the lepers and proclaim the Kingdom (Luke 10:1-9)
He calls us to be holy as He is holy (1 Peter 1:15)
He calls us to be overcomers (Rev Chapters 2 & 3)
He calls us to take up our cross and deny ourselves (Luke 9:23)
He calls us to walk in the same way He walked (1 John 2:6)
And as we start to do these things, we become those whom the Father is seeking. We become worshipers.

The reality is that we cannot do any of these things by ourselves. The only power for permanent change is through the action of the Holy Spirit in our lives.
Jesus calls us to this life, and then says He will send the Holy Spirit to give us the power to live it.
This is absolutely incredible! The Father shows us what He wants, knows we can not do it, but then provides the solution and power so that we can. And then He says "well done good and faithful servant".
And we did less than nothing to deserve it.

Have you noticed that we do not have the ability to change ourselves?
There are a myriad of self-help programs available in bookshops, magazines, seminars and on the internet.
New Age and Mysticism Gurus promote their theories and programs;
Alternative Lifestyle Experts convince us to live in ways which are not normal;
Doctors and councillors, Psychiatrists and Therapists, advertise their success stories and they all clamour for our dollars.

At the very best, their relief is only temporary. Then their "solution" becomes disappointing and brings disillusionment.
That is because they are "self" help programs. Self, and the councillor and the program get the glory. Self is transient and unreliable.
This is not the solution we need, we need a permanent change.
We seek and we need permanent transformation in our lives.
The good news is, transformation is available for everyone. Permanent results and rewards are guaranteed, but there is a condition, a cost.

The condition is this: we must do it God's way.
Then, He gets the glory. And rightly so. Only God has provided the remedy for our sin.
The remedy is this; to live in His will, with our life fully

yielded and surrendered to Jesus and powered by The Holy Spirit.

To begin this process, we must be born again.
To continue this process, we must become a living sacrifice.

God wants us to lay our lives on the altar as a living sacrifice, which is a reasonable response to what Jesus did for us.

(Romans 12:1)
This is the cost - everything we are.

The term "living sacrifice" is an interesting one.
In the Old Covenant framework, a sacrifice was killed, put on the altar and consumed. There was nothing left. No-one had ever conceived of a "living" sacrifice before, because a sacrifice was always dead and expended.

So when Paul writes to the Christians in Rome and introduces the term "living sacrifice", he introduces a very strange and impossible mix of words. An oxymoron.
But then as he continues his discourse, Paul spends a lot of time explaining what he means. The rest of Chapter 12, all of Chapters 13 and 14, and the beginning of Chapter 15, all show what Paul means by a "living sacrifice".

Romans 12:1 and Romans 12:2 are not separate verses in Paul's mind. But we have split them up like that, so we miss what Paul is really saying by dissecting his thoughts in that way. Romans Chapter 11 to Romans Chapter 15 are all part of one main thought, about which Paul is writing to his readers.

Dear Saints, Paul is talking about what our life in Jesus looks like. He is talking about worship.

Then to finish off his letter to the saints in Rome, Paul shows that Jesus is our prime example of what it means to be a real worshiper.

Paul starts his letter to the Romans with a description of what happens when people worship false gods:

...because they exchanged the truth about God for a lie and worshiped and served the creature rather than the Creator, who is blessed forever! Amen. (Rom 1:25)(reading the rest of Romans chapter 1 will give you the context)

And then he finishes his letter by describing how Jesus shows us the perfect example of worship:

For Christ did not please himself,but as it is written, "The reproaches of those who reproached you fell on me." (Rom 15:3)(read all of Romans 15:1-13 to see the context.

Note that Paul also refers to 2 Samuel, Psalms, Deuteronomy, Psalms and Isaiah)

Paul is describing the life of a worshiper under the New Covenant. He is describing the nature of true worship.

Paul starts this letter to the Romans by describing the nature and results of false worship, and finishes it with a detailed explanation of real worship. This is what the Father is seeking.

Oh, the depth of the riches and wisdom and knowledge of God!(Romans 11:33)

The New Testament is a comprehensive worship manual. Let us change our focus from music, to the way we live our lives.

8. Worship and God's Covenants

In Chapter 5 we saw that there is a fundamental shift in our relationship to the Father from the Old Testament to the New Testament. This shift also radically affects our understanding of worship, as introduced by Jesus when he explained to the woman at the well in Samaria what true worship really was.

"But the hour is coming, and is now here, when the true worshipers will worship the Fatherin spirit and truth, for the Father is seeking such people to worship him." (John 4:23)

Jesus' statement also implies that up until this time, true worship was not available in the way the Father is seeking. This is simply because until Jesus came, they did not and could not, have the relationship with the Father as we now can. In fact, that relationship was lost in the Garden of Eden when Adam sinned.

In order to more fully understand this seismic shift in the nature of our restored relationship with the Father, it is really helpful to understand the nature of the New Covenant. This is what we will explore in this Chapter.

I am indebted to David Pawson's teaching on Covenants, which I consider to be the finest and most comprehensive on this subject.[21]

In the Bible, the word "covenant" means something very specific, and it is quite different from an agreement, a contract or a promise. A covenant is not a prayer or a dedication or a statement of intent, but something much more powerful, binding and permanent.
The covenants in Scripture were never man's idea, but they always contained statements from God about what He would or would not do.

A covenant in Scripture was always initiated by God on His terms, with His conditions. We can accept it or reject it, but there is no place for discussion. A covenant is much more than a promise or a dedication, but is a universal and lasting statement of what God will do. It is always sealed with a significant sign, and the strongest and most binding of all seals is blood, because the life is in the blood.[22]

Note that here we are looking at God's Covenants as made from God to man, not an agreement made by men between each other. We would call such an agreement a

contract, but in the old Hebrew context, they did not have that word as we do today.
There is an equivalent Hebrew word *berith,*which, in the English, is translated as "covenant."[23]It can be confusing if we do not understand the context.

The nearest thing we have to the Biblical term "covenant" is a person's Last Will And Testament. This Will in legal terms, which is also called a testament or a covenant, is irrevocable and lasting but only comes into effect upon the death of the person who made the Will.

Our Bibles are divided into the Old Testament and the New Testament. It is somewhat unfortunate that this terminology of "Old and New" is used, because it is not an accurate description of God's Word, the Scriptures as breathed by the Holy Spirit.

We tend to think that the Old Testament is how God used to be, and the New Testament describes how God is now. No, God never changed, but the potential of our relationship to Him has.

The New Testament could indeed be called the New Will, or the New Covenant. But the Old Testament contains four other covenants, and of those, all are still current except for one, the only covenant which is old and superseded.

These five covenants in Scripture are all initiated by God, with stipulations and a distinct purpose to fulfil.

They are known as the Noahic Covenant, the Abrahamic Covenant, the Mosaic Covenant, the Davidic Covenant and the Messianic Covenant. Each covenant is named after the person with whom God made the covenant.

We are only going to look at the Mosaic Covenant in detail here, because this is the one which contains information about worship, and this is the only covenant which is obsolete.

Here is a summary of the five covenants contained in Scripture.

Covenant:	Applies to:	Sealed with:	Purpose:	Duration:	Reference:	Conditional**
Noahic:	All people	Rainbow	Survival	Until the earth ends	Gen 9:11-17	No
Abrahamic:	Israel	Circumcision	Selection	Eternal	Gen 17:19-21	No
Mosaic:	Israel	Animals blood	Conduct	Superseded	Exo 34:0-28	Yes
Davidic:	All people	God's Word	Sovereignty	Eternal	2Sam 7:1-17	No
Messianic:	All people	Jesus' Blood	Salvation	New, Eternal	Heb 8:1-10:25 *	Yes

* (In Hebrews, there are references to the OT prophesies about the New Covenant. It is worthwhile looking these up for yourself.

** Note also, that the Noahic, Abrahamic and Davidic Covenants are unconditional - God will do this regardless of our response. However, a response is required in the Messianic Covenant, which replaces the Mosaic Covenant.)

It is important to notice about these Covenants, that there is only one which has been superseded (old). That is the Mosaic Covenant. The other four are permanent.
Hebrews talks a lot about how this (Mosaic) covenant has been replaced with the New Covenant. The New Covenant is the Messianic Covenant, and was established and came into effect when Jesus died.
This is just like a person's Last Will and Testament. If someone makes a will, and then before they die they make a new one, then by law, the most recent Will is the one which is in force. All wills before that are superseded and obsolete.

So it is very important for us to understand when we read the Old Testament, which parts belong to which covenant.

Misunderstanding of the Covenants has led to many doctrinal divisions, error and in some cases, persecution.
For instance if we don't understand that the Abrahamic Covenant is permanent, then that leads to "Replacement Theology", which claims that the Church has now replaced Israel. That is incorrect of course, as Paul points out very eloquently in Romans Chapter 11. (As well as Galations 3, Hebrews 8)

I ask, then, has God rejected his people? By no means! (Rom 11:1)

The Mosaic Covenant contains all the laws, rules for conduct and living, all given to Moses by God Himself. Tragically, the Scribes and Pharisees added many other rules and laws to the things that God had given. These are referred to as "hedge laws", and were made up to try to protect people from breaking the fundamental laws. The fundamental laws which made up the Mosaic Covenant were the 10 commandments and over 600 others as found in Exodus, Leviticus and Deuteronomy.

The "hedge laws" became a heavy burden, and it was impossible to even know them all. (Some estimate thousands of laws!) This led to the people being manipulated by the Pharisees and kept under fear and bondage, all in God's name.

It was a form of control and it still happens today.

Legalism is produced by absorbing any or all of the Mosaic Covenant laws into our "church life". Unfortunately, many churches adopt these rules, and one of the Churches in the New Testament, the Church in Galatia, tried to do this. Paul was very strong in his letter to the Galations, condemning every aspect of this mixture and compromise. Paul's letter is as relevant today as it was when he wrote it.

For freedom Christ has set us free; stand firm therefore, and do not submit again to a yoke of slavery. Look: I, Paul, say to you that if you accept circumcision, Christ will be of no advantage to you. I testify again to every man who accepts circumcision that he is obligated to keep the whole law. (Galations 5:1)

It is hard to just pick just one verse from Galations to completely illustrate what Paul is saying, because he is referring all the way through his letter, to those who would go back to the law (of Moses) to try to live their lives now in the New Covenant with Jesus.

In Paul's second letter to the Corinthian church, he makes a dramatic life and death comparison between the Mosaic and the New Covenants. He explains it this way:

"For the letter kills, but the Spirit gives life. Now if the ministry of death, carved in letters on stone, came with such glory that the Israelites could not gaze at Moses' face because of its glory, which was being brought to an end, will not the ministry of the Spirit have even more glory?"
(2 Corinthians 3:6-9)

Paul describes the Mosaic Covenant as being a "ministry of death". And even that was glorious and splendid. But it pales into insignificance by comparison with the New Covenant, which being powered by the Holy Spirit within us, far exceeds the splendour and glory of the Old.

Truth is no longer viewed from afar with the types and shadows of the Old Covenant. Truth is now visible, demonstrated and brought to our lives by Jesus.
Jesus IS the truth.
The Mosaic Covenant was like a travel brochure that pointed to the Kingdom Of God. Now, we have been

born into that Kingdom and live there by the Grace and Truth that came with Jesus.

Truth did not come until Jesus came. We did not know Truth before that. Until He came, people lived in the shadow of the good things to come.[24]

For the law was given through Moses; grace and truth came through Jesus Christ. (John 1:17)

This also applies to our expression of worship to the Father. Any hint of legalism, rules, or adopting the Old Covenant ways of worship, excludes us from worshiping the Father "in spirit and in truth". The Mosaic Covenant is not the truth, it was only ever a shadow of the truth which came in Jesus. The Old Covenant brought death.

Jesus described truth and worshiping the Father in spirit, as being the essence of the New Covenant in John 4:23

(true worshipers will worship the Father in Spirit and in truth).
To live there, means putting aside all the old rules and methods.
They were types and shadows of the reality of real worship of the Father.

The Galations were legalistically putting rules from the Old Covenant on their walk as Christians.
Paul had to write a very stern letter to them, rebuking them for trying to live again in the Old Covenant.

The Scribes and Pharisees had for a very long time, placed very heavy burdens on the people.
They added literally, thousands more laws to the laws of Moses.

This is why Jesus referred to them as hypocrites and vipers, among other things.
Jesus deliberately broke many of their man-made rules, to show that their rules were of no power or significance. However, Jesus kept ALL of God's laws precisely and completely, as no one else had ever done. Jesus is the fulfilment of the Law.

Jesus is the Fulfilment

We have seen how the Old Testament contains many images, types and shadows of things to come, which are fulfilled in the New Testament.

When Jesus came, He fulfilled everything in the Old Testament that was said about Him, and also established the New Covenant by shedding his blood. (Matt 26:26-29, Mark 14:24, Luke 22:20)

The New Covenant, The New Testament, The New Will, is now in effect since Jesus' death.

It is legal that a person's Will does not come into effect until the person dies. That is so with the New Covenant Jesus came to establish. He initiated it with His death and sealed it with His blood. The blood covenant is the most powerful and binding type of Covenant in Scripture.

Paul, in his first letter to the Corinthians, gives us a record of the beginning of the New Covenant:

For I received from the Lord what I also delivered to you, that the Lord Jesus on the night when he was betrayed took bread, and when he had given thanks, he broke it, and said, "This is my body, which is for you. Do this in remembrance of me."
In the same way also he took the cup, after supper, saying, "This cup is the new covenant in my blood. Do this, as often as you drink it, in remembrance of me." (1 Cor 11:23-25)

Jesus' death and the shedding of His blood, placed the Messianic Covenant into effect.

These words are exactly what Jesus said at the last supper, which is very interesting because Paul was not there. Paul said, "I received from the Lord…" Jesus Himself, personally shared this with Paul, emphasising the

importance of celebrating the Lord's Supper.
The beginning of the New Covenant is so significant, that the Lord said to do this as often as we would, so that we remember what He has done for us.

Now that the Messianic Covenant has come, the Mosaic Covenant has been replaced, superseded, put away, discarded.
In other words, nothing in the Mosaic Covenant applies to Israel anymore, and neither does it apply to us, since we have been grafted into the Vine. (See Romans Chapters 9 - 11)
Ezekiel, Jeremiah and Isaiah all prophesied of the establishment of the New Covenant.

"Behold, the days are coming, declares the LORD, when I will make a new covenant with the house of Israel and the house of Judah, not like the covenant that I made with their fathers on the day when I took them by the hand to bring them out of the land of Egypt, my covenant that they broke, though I was their husband, declares the LORD.
For this is the covenant that I will make with the house of Israel after those days, declares the LORD: I will put my law within them, and I will write it on their hearts. And I will be their God, and they shall be my people. (Jeremiah 31:31-33) - (Emphasis mine).
(Also see Ezekiel 36:26-27 and Isaiah 59:21)

The New Covenant meant that God was actually going to deal with our motives - our hearts.
The New Covenant is not like the Old Covenant.
Ezekiel puts it this way:

And I will give you a new heart, and a new spirit I will put within you. And I will remove the heart of stone from your flesh and give you a heart of flesh. And I will put my Spirit within you, and cause you to walk in my statutes and be careful to obey my rules. (Eze 26:26-27)

Jesus amplified the operation of the New Covenant in Matthew Chapters 5 and 6 where He showed people that they were incapable of even thinking the right way. But under the New Covenant, He has sent the Holy Spirit to dwell in us, lead us, guide and teach us how to be the people who truly walk in His ways. The Holy Spirit gives us the power to be able to live in the New Covenant.
Not because we HAVE to, but because we WANT to. Our heart of stone is replaced by a heart of flesh - duty has been replaced by delight.

The Mosaic Covenant was given to Moses by God on a mountain. It was written on stone.
The Messianic Covenant was given to us by Jesus on a mountain. It was written on hearts.

To use computing technology as an example, the old operating system for our pentium-powered laptop has been superseded by a new operating system. The new system requires new hardware and it requires the old operating system to be deleted. It is no use anymore.
Don't try to run the old operating system on your new computer, it will not work. And trying to make it work using patches and fixes is a frustrating and futile pursuit.

Now that we have looked very briefly at the establishment of the New Covenant, let us look at some significant things that change because of the operation of the New Covenant. There are many.

For instance, circumcision (of the flesh) has been replaced by circumcision of the heart
But a Jew is one inwardly, and circumcision is a matter of the heart, by the Spirit, not by the letter. His praise is not from man but from God. (Rom 2:29)

Tithing has been replaced by giving
The point is this: whoever sows sparingly will also reap sparingly, and whoever sows bountifully will also reap bountifully. Each one must give as he has decided in his heart, not reluctantly or under compulsion, for God loves a cheerful giver. (2 Cor 9:6-7)

Animal sacrifice and altar worship has been replaced by sacrifice of ourselves

I appeal to you therefore, brothers, by the mercies of God, to present your bodies as a living sacrifice, holy and acceptable to God, which is your spiritual worship. (Rom 12:1)

These are all radically significant changes for the Jews, to whom Paul was speaking. They were difficult to accept, until the Holy Spirit brought the understanding of these changes to their hearts.

When Jesus died and the veil of the temple was torn in two, God was showing that the ways they had been worshiping were now over, and a new and living way had replaced the old and dead way.

He was establishing a completely new framework for worship, which involved open access to the Father, through the blood of Jesus.

Here was the establishment and beginning of the Messianic Covenant, something that would completely satisfy God's requirements, and fulfil all of our desires.

Here is a small summary of some of the things which have been superseded when Jesus established the New Covenant.

The New Covenant		
Old Covenant	Superseded By	Reference
Tithing	Giving	2 Cor 9:6-7
Circumcision	Purifying the heart	Rom 2:1-29
All Mosaic Laws	Laws written on our hearts	Hebrews 8: 1-13; Gal 5:1-14
Blood sacrifice	Jesus' one-time offering	Hebrews 9:1-28
Temple worship	The Body Of Christ	1 Cor 6:19-20
Levitical Priesthood	Priesthood of all believers	1 Peter 2:9-12
Passover	Communion	1 Cor 11:17-34

In Hebrews 10 we see this about the New Covenant:

Therefore, brothers, since we have confidence to enter the holy places by the blood of Jesus,
by the new and living (not the old and dead) way that he opened for us through the curtain, that is, through his flesh, and since we have a great priest over the house of God, let us draw near with a true heart in full assurance of faith, with our hearts sprinkled clean from an evil conscience and our bodies washed with pure water. (Hebrews 10:19-22)

It means that the old rules, laws, procedures, customs and rituals were now superseded by the New Covenant that Jesus established in His blood.
The Old was law, which brought death. The New is life in Jesus.
The Old was bondage and guilt, the New is freedom and liberty.

And so it is that we see we have been set free from the old rules, laws, bondages and trying to work out our own righteousness by keeping the rules. That is how it was under the Law of the Old Covenant, which was impossible to keep.

The problem is, that although life in the Spirit sets us free from the entirety of the law, it requires us laying down our lives to the Lordship of Jesus.
We are not ours anymore, we have been bought with a fiercely expensive price, and our response can only simply be, to submit ourselves to Jesus - to His rulership, and to His complete will.
Then Jesus promises that by losing our life we will find it and by dying to self we can live for Him.

Now this is a problem for us because we don't like to give up our old ways. The law is predictable, clinical and concise. Living in the Spirit is unpredictable, unknown and challenging.
So it is with worship.
We like to be in charge, like to know exactly how, when and where, and we like to see predictable results.

There is a tragic illustration in Scripture of this.
We discussed a little in Chapter 3, about the time that King David re-captured the Ark of God's Presence from the Philistines. He brought it back with much ceremony and

sacrifice.
However, the place to which David brought the Ark, was not the place anybody expected it to be.
David brought the Ark back and placed it in a tent, which he had pitched for it in Jerusalem.

The Ark always represented the tangible presence of God, and to place it in a tent meant that there was open access to God's presence. In a symbolic sense, David was prophesying of the New Covenant which would be established.

At this time, Moses Tabernacle had also been rebuilt on Mt Gibeon near Jerusalem. It would have had a Holy place and a Holy of Holies where the Ark was placed, as they journeyed in the wilderness.
The priests and Levites were still offering sacrifices and worshiping at the Tabernacle of Moses on Mount Gibeon when David brought the Ark back, but God's presence was not there.
God's presence was in the tent in Jerusalem.

So Moses' system of Levitical worship and its rituals of sacrifice and cleansing, were in operation at the same time that David and others were worshiping at the Ark in Jerusalem.
This is a simple but very sad, illustration of how we also

like to hang onto our old traditions. They are comfortable and familiar.

The Priests and Levites were still worshiping according to their form, but without God's presence.
Trying to duplicate Moses' Tabernacle order of worship is not part of the New Covenant.
And neither is David's Tabernacle, or Solomon's temple.

Many of our gatherings as believers are devoid of the Presence and Power of God, because we follow the ways of the Old Covenant.
So much of our worship is in vain because it is not in truth, but based on the shadow of the Old Covenant. The Old Covenant is not the Truth, Jesus is. Truth and Grace came through Jesus.

So much of our service is devoid of life, because it is based on law rather than Life in Christ Jesus.

God's presence is no longer represented by an Ark or a specific place, because He now dwells within us by the Holy Spirit.

We have seen how worship is about the way we live our lives before God, not about music, not about adhering to any form or formula.
The big shift in our thinking needs to come as we consider what worship really is, and what the Father is seeking.

The heart of the matter is this: We cannot duplicate the Old Covenant ways of doing things in our life as disciples, and expect to live in the New Covenant.
By duplicating the worship of Moses' Tabernacle or David's Tabernacle, we place ourselves under the operation of the Old Covenant. It does not work and is not valid anymore.

We cannot expect the freedom and fullness of New Covenant living, and still cling to the formula and method of the Old Covenant.
Things such as Tithing, Circumcision, Temple worship, Ten Commandments, Sabbath rules and regulations and so much more. Those things belong to the worn out, superseded and discarded Mosaic Covenant.

'But the hour is coming, and is now here, when the true worshipers will worship the Father in spirit and truth, for the Father is seeking such people to worship him." (John 4:23)

We have not discussed much yet about "in spirit and truth", but that is coming soon.

9. Tradgedy in Worship

Tragedy surrounds us in this life.

Many have had close relatives die before their time. It is a horrific, life changing tragedy to have to bury your own child.
It is a tragedy when a parent walks away from their family, or children walk away from their parents.
It is a tragedy when war dislocates and decimates families and even whole countries; there is no coming back from that.
But I believe there is a bigger tragedy, and that is when people live in deception, thinking that how they are living and what they are doing is the truth, when they are actually believing and living a lie. This is a much bigger tragedy because it effects them for eternity.

Jesus, Paul and other New Testament writers warn us of deception, of thinking that we are doing the right thing, when actually we are not.
In the first few verses of Matthew 24, when Jesus' disciples ask Him about the signs of the last days, Jesus warns them five times about deception.

This is one of the strongest signs that we are indeed living in the last of the last days.

Deception is rampant, first of all in the Church and second in the world. We can hardly believe anything in the media anymore, as we see rampant propaganda and manipulation. But false doctrines and manipulation, along with New Age thinking, are also endemic in the church.
It is so incredibly important that we are constantly in the Word, which is the only way to avoid deception.

Here are quotes from Jesus:
"See that no one leads you astray", "…they will lead many astray", "…many will fall away and betray one another", "..false prophets will lead many astray", "…the love of many will grow cold" (Matt 24:4,5,10,11,12)

Let's take a small side track here and investigate something that is a very effective strategy of the enemy, but is not always easy to recognise. It is called the strategy of the Fifth Column.

During the Spanish Civil War of 1936, General Emilio Mola and his supporters marched on Madrid, to take the city. Mola stated that he had four columns of troops approaching the city, from each of the compass directions. But then he stated he also had a fifth column of troops stationed inside the city.

The fifth column were hidden troops disguised inside the city, who would join the four other ranks of soldiers as they marched on the city.

The enemy's strategy is to have a "fifth column" installed inside the Church, so that when the assault happens on a larger scale, the Church will simultaneously be attacked from within.

External and internal forces are at work to destroy the Church. The internal force, is largely a force of deception.

We are not of those who fall back. We know which side is going to win, and we are bold to be those overcomers in Jesus name who will prevail, even at the cost of our lives. This is a great encouragement to endure, as Revelation tells us. It is also another encouragement to be constantly in His Word. We are encouraged several times in Revelation, to perservere.

Here is a call for the endurance of the saints, those who keep the commandments of God and their faith in Jesus. (Rev 14:12)

We Will Give Account

We all must die and face the Master and give account for the way we lived. Jesus is very straightforward about that.

"Not everyone who says to me, 'Lord, Lord,' will enter the kingdom of heaven, but the one who does the will of my Father who is in

heaven. On that day many will say to me, 'Lord, Lord, did we not prophesy in your name, and cast out demons in your name, and do many mighty works in your name?' And then will I declare to them, 'I never knew you; depart from me, you workers of lawlessness. (Matt 7:21-23. Also Luke 13:26-27)

Jesus is not trying to create fear and panic, but to help us evaluate objectively where we stand in our relationship with Him. Jesus is speaking to us from the perspective of Eternity, not just in the present moment. The only real and sure protection is the Word of God, the Scriptures that stand unmovable, objective and eternal. We must as disciples, be in that word constantly.

Deception usually starts with a mixture of truth and error. Deception starts small and ends up big.

Satan is, and always has been, a liar. The Bible calls him the "father of lies". He lies to us about ourselves. ("you're no good at that; you'll never succeed; you will never get free of that; you are a failure", you brought this on yourself and you deserve it…")

Have you ever noticed that satan always talks to you in the first person?

He lies to us about our beliefs, he lies to us about our practices, and he lies to us about our destiny.

These are all common and demeaning lies that people believe and receive about themselves.

The enemy lies to us constantly.
But the biggest lie the devil has ever convinced people to believe, is that he doesn't exist.
And there are many that believe that lie and live accordingly.

Another big lie the enemy tells is that what you are doing is right, when in fact it is not in line with Scripture. The enemy says, "this is the way, you are doing this right…" when in fact you do not realise it is incorrect. This is deception and Jesus also warns us about that. In fact as we have seen, five times in the beginning of Matthew Chapter 24, Jesus warns us believers about deception. A tragic deception, is for us to believe we are doing the right thing, when in fact the very opposite is the truth.
This is the enemy at work.

How can we insulate ourselves against deception? By being constantly in the Word.
If we are constantly immersed in the Truth, we will automatically recognise deception when it is presented to us.

Worship is exclusive

How that relates to worship is all encompassing, because it is the foundational thing that satan has wanted since the beginning of the deception in the Garden of Eden.

Satan wants us to worship him, not God.
If he cannot get you to worship him directly, he will try to get you to worship anything but God.
In Isaiah we have God's record of what satan said to Him, and therefore God cast satan out of Heaven.

This is the five "I Wills" of satan.

Here is God talking to Satan:
You said in your heart,
'I will ascend to heaven; above the stars of God
I will set my throne on high;
I will sit on the mount of assembly in the far reaches of the north;
I will ascend above the heights of the clouds;
I will make myself like the Most High.'
(Isaiah 14:13-14)

This is also how satan tempted Jesus in the wilderness, before Jesus began his full-time ministry. "I will give you all of this if you bow down and worship me". This is a cunning approach, but one the enemy uses on us still.

Again, the devil took him to a very high mountain and showed him all the kingdoms of the world and their glory. And he said to him, "All these I will give you, if you will fall down and worship me." Then Jesus said to him, "Be gone, Satan! For it is written, "'You shall worship the Lord your God and him only shall you serve."' (Matt 4:8-10)

We see here the exclusivity that Jesus displays when He says we should ONLY worship and serve God and no other. Indeed, worshiping anything else places our focus on things of the enemy's kingdom.
Nothing else can ever satisfy us. God's claim on our worship is exclusive.

The tragedy in worship is that that we can be deceived into worshiping something that is not God. We can even be deceived into worshiping him in a manner that is not the way He has described. We must worship in spirit and in truth. We will see a bit more about that later.

"Praise and Worship" is now an official genre of music in the world's eyes.
In fact we have seen from the Scripture, that Worship, and Praise are not necessarily linked to music at all. Yet the worldly "Christian" commercial marketing machine has us believing that the music in the "P&W" genre is an authentic expression of those things to God, when it really is not what God desires at all.
How could we think for a moment, that what "The Father is seeking", is somehow contained in the latest songs of "praise and worship" from the Christian marketing machine? If we subscribe to this, then our praise, and

indeed our very worship is greatly impoverished, unfocussed and even impotent.
This is actually a pervasive phenomenon in the body of Christ. It diffuses our focus from the power and energy of real worship, to that which is anything and everything else. This is enemy deception.

Let us look for a moment at a major expression of "worship" that exists today.
I am going to call this phenomenon, "Blackbox Worship".

When you walk into many church services today, the whole space is painted black. The stage is black except for the spotlights that are on the musicians, perhaps with moving colours in the background, and maybe smoke and laser lights. There is a bit of controlled lighting on the audience.

There are many examples of this Blackbox Worship readily available on the internet.
The music is polished and well rehearsed, designed to excite emotions and generate enthusiasm. The songs are well known and played frequently, promoted by the Christian marketing machine. The music is LOUD and pulsing, quite often at dangerous levels. (close to 110 decibels for those who understand the terminology. That is about the loudness you would experience if you stand behind a jet plane taking off. It will cause hearing damage).

I remember going to one such event back in the early 2000's, in Castle Hill in Sydney Australia. The featured speaker was Bill Johnson from Bethel, and the music was very loud. I happened to have my sound level meter with me and measured the sound level at around 110 decibels. The kick drum sounded like a cannon going off, almost loud enough to adjust your heartbeat. We had to go outside until the music had finished (for an hour or so), and stood around with dozens of other people who had also escaped from the audio onslaught they called "praise and worship".

Blackbox Worship is promoted as the gold standard of Praise and Worship music today in churches and organisations all over the world. Unfortunately, this does not line up with what the Scripture describes as Worship, or what the Scripture describes as Praise.

What Blackbox Worship does line up with however, is the majority of rock concerts throughout the world.
U2, Rolling Stones, Metallica, all the major concerts, have these Blackbox Worship ingredients.
And the audience worships the rock heroes. Hands are raised, emotions are stirred and the musicians are idolised.
Some church music is so similar to rock concerts, it is hard to tell the difference.

The emotional influence of music is well known, well researched and studied.[25]The concerts - and "praise and worship" sessions - are clinically engineered to manipulate people's emotions for a desired effect. In church, giving is increased after the music, listening is heightened when the emotions are thus stirred, and there is a very real element of emotional and mental conditioning that is associated with this music. "Altar calls" have music that stirs the emotions and "helps" in you coming forward.

It is manipulation, and music is a very powerful tool for this because of the way it impacts the emotions. Music has been used this way for decades.

Here is a quote from Watchman Nee:

"Let us remember that all works done through emotion are questionable and transient. In the work done through the power of the Holy Spirit, man does not need to exert his own strength nor do anything by himself. If a work is done by soul strength, one has to exert lots of energy and employ numerous methods such as weeping, shouting, jumping, incessant singing of choruses, or the telling of a number of moving stories. For the employment of these methods serves no other purpose than that of trying to stir up the audience."

Watchman Nee. The Latent Power Of The Soul. Copyright ©1972 Christian Fellowship Publishers, Inc. New York. Free pdf download, page 40. https://all-med.net/pdf/latent-power-of-the-soul/

There is a new phenomenon in church music today that has been termed "soaking" music.
It is designed as background music that you play for an hour or more, and pray and simply focus your thoughts on the Lord, or just let your thoughts roam.
Unfortunately this is nothing but a New Age mind control technique, and listeners will often mistake their heightened emotions produced this way, as the "moving of the Spirit".

I once asked our home group to see if they could tell the difference between what was New Age music and what was Christian "soaking" music. I played some You Tube clips of "soaking "music back to back with New Age meditation music and asked people to say which was which.
No one could tell the difference, and in fact chose incorrectly most of the time. The "soaking" music clips I chose were from Bethel and Elevation. People could not distinguish the difference, even though our home group contained some more mature believers.
You can easily test this for yourself.[26]

The New Age has infiltrated our churches in music as well as doctrine, and we haven't even noticed.

It has always been satan's desire to control people, and one of the tools he uses is music. He has convinced many, perhaps a large portion of the Body Of Christ, that what

they do when they sing in church is "worship", when the Scripture plainly shows that this is not so.
The comment that people make when they say, "The worship was great today", usually means that the songs induced emotions which they enjoyed.
This is not the worship that is described in the Bible.

Remember Abraham's response, Job's response and David's response? Those responses are described vividly as responses of worship, but they are acts of the will, not emotional responses to a song.

Many unscriptural phrases abound today such as, "Let's have some worship", or Didn't we have a great time of worship today?", or "The worship is really intense in that church", or "I love the way they worship".
Unfortunately, this is not what Jesus says the Father is looking for.
Our focus has been changed from what the Father wants, to something that makes us feel good and is essentially an emotional response to the music.
This is a typical and standard enemy tactic. It is a deception and we have become focused on the wrong thing.

One thing that should be particularly noticed as we study Scripture on this topic, is that most of the time, "worship" is a verb. It is an action that we make towards God.

In the summary of the characteristics of worship in Chapter 3, the elements of worship are all verbs. Bowing, sacrificing, offering, praying, declaring, are all action words, verbs.
Very occasionally we see worship referred to as a noun, but we never see worship referred to as an adjective. In the New Covenant you never see a "worship service" or a "worship team", nor in fact a "worship ministry".

The New Testament is quite devoid of any mention of worship in connection with ministry.
But you would think by looking at the church today, that the worship leader would be one of the main persons and ministries mentioned in the New Testament.
The worship team is noticeably absent from the New Testament. There is no such ministry mentioned.
There are plenty of other ministries mentioned, but not that one.
We have lost our focus.

I am going to say something that will ruffle some feathers, or perhaps even offend some. I was also offended by this in the past.

There is no such thing in the New Testament as a person who is a "Worship Leader".

Regrettably, I functioned in the role of a "worship leader" for many years, not understanding that this is not what God is looking for. I had replaced the New Testament call of the Father to worship Him, with the Old Testament form and formula, which led to routine and ritual. The end point of that can often be legalism, which simply implies that "if you are not doing it this way, you are not in the spirit".

And this is because I did not read the Scriptures for myself and analyse them properly. I analysed the Scriptures with a bias, and had an agenda as if looking through a coloured filter.

We need to take off our sunglasses and put on real Son-Glasses.

One of the functions of the Holy Spirit, is to lead us in worship, and He always focuses on the Father.

I have come to understand that anything that gets in the way of the Holy Spirit and His work, grieves Him.

We have put ourselves as "worship leaders" in the place of of the Holy Spirit, and He simply backs away. Then we mistake our emotional response to the music and the teaching, as the "moving of the Holy Spirit".

When we put on a You Tube clip of the latest song from the CCLI[28]worship list, or think that our participation in singing along with a staged performance is "worshiping the

Lord", we are participating in the Christian Marketing Machine's mantra of "worship". That is not what the Bible describes as worship.

There is nothing wrong with listening to spiritual songs from Christian artists, if they stimulate your thoughts and emotions to give praise to God, but we must not come to the conclusion that this is "worship". That is a long way from what the Father is seeking.

What our emotional response is in fact, is a soulish reaction to the received input. The response comes from our soul, as we will see in the next chapter, but we mistake it as coming from our spirit. We must worship the Father in spirit and in truth, not in soul and truth.

If you grieve the Holy Spirit, He will leave.

Oh how patient and gracious is God toward us who are so frail!
He is so patient with us, and so kind.

The Lord is not slow to fulfil his promise as some count slowness, but is patient toward you, not wishing that any should perish, but that all should reach repentance. (2 Peter 3:9)

'However, You bore with them for many years,
And admonished them by Your Spirit through Your prophets,
Yet they would not give ear.
Therefore You gave them into the hand of the peoples of the lands.
'Nevertheless, in Your great compassion You did not make an end of them or forsake them,
For You are a gracious and compassionate God. (Nehemiah 9:30-31)

But this will not always be so.
In Acts we see the Holy Spirit actually killing Ananias and Sapphira for lying to Him, which brought great fear and respect on the early church. I believe the days are coming when we will see such things again, especially as the days approach of the return of the Lord Jesus. We need such reverence and fear for the LORD in our daily walk.

Let us not presume that we can put ourselves in the place of the Holy Spirit and pretend to "lead people in worship". That is His role not ours, and to do anything else is to simply act from ignorance about the nature of true worship. To assume that we can do something which only belongs to the Holy Spirit is a gross misunderstanding of worship, and an even greater misunderstanding of the role of the Holy Spirit in our lives.

We have seen that real worship is not particularly about a corporate experience.

It is more intensely personal than anything else. It grieves the Holy Spirit when we put someone between us and God. That is the Old Testament model of the Priesthood, as typified by Moses' Tabernacle and Solomon's Temple.
The Old Testament model of worship is part of the Mosaic Covenant, and is obsolete.

We know this is so, because when God gave Moses the Ten Commandments He also gave Moses the detailed plans for the Tabernacle.[27]This was also continued in Solomon's temple worship format.
The Mosaic Covenant has been replaced by the Messianic Covenant - the reality of a promise of much better things.

The Mosaic Covenant is the picture, the type, the travel brochure.

The Messianic Covenant is the reality of life in Jesus.

Jesus Is Better Than Moses	*(Heb. 3:1-4:13)*
Jesus leads us into the Rest of God	*(Heb. 3:1-4:13)*
Jesus is a better high priest	*(Heb. 4:14-7:28)*
Jesus introduced a better Covenant	*(Heb. 8:1-9:28)*
Jesus provided a better sacrifice	*(Heb. 10:1-39)*

"...and to Jesus, the mediator of a new covenant, and to the sprinkled blood that speaks a better word than the blood of Abel. (Heb 12:24)

Unfortunately, so much of our modern expressions of "worship", are simply a direct import from the Old Covenant. It is new wine in old wineskins, and it is not what the Father is seeking.

People believe they are worshiping when they attend a "worship service" and sing "worship songs". The Father is not seeking people who will participate in a setlist of songs off the CCLI[28]top 100.

The Father is seeking those who will put their lives on the altar every day and submit to His Lordship.
That is the reality of true Worship.

Jesus used the phrase "new wine in old wineskins" to refer to the fact that the things which are new, cannot be put into an old container. He also used the illustration of a piece of new cloth sewn onto an old garment in the same context. (Matthew 9:16-17, Luke 5:33-39)
Jesus' illustration, is referring to His miracles, healings and other works that He did and was doing. The Pharisees, as usual, complained a lot about Him doing those things.

In the context of the complete discourse from Jesus, it is easy to see that He is referring to the difference between

the Old Covenant and the New Covenant.
The things from the Old Covenant (Mosaic), cannot be contained by the New Covenant (Messianic). The New Covenant needs a new container.

It was clear to the Scribes and Pharisees that Jesus was not adhering to any of their man-made laws, traditions and customs. But what they could not see at that time, was that Jesus was actually going to abolish the Old Covenant and introduce the New Covenant. The disciples saw that later, after Jesus died and rose again.

Now that we have looked at what worship clearly is not, let's look at the ways we can really worship God in our daily lives.
For the Father Himself is seeking this kind of person, those who will worship Him in spirit and in truth. (John4:23)

10. Worship in Our Daily Life

In order to really understand truth, we must look at Jesus because He said He was the Way and the Truth and the Life

(John 14:6). We also know from John 1:1 and Revelation 19:, that Jesus is the "Word".
So we also need to pay careful attention to what the Word says, if we are to discover the Truth.

We have seen that worship as described in the Bible, is not what we typically observe as worship in the church today.
We have also seen that praise has many more dimensions than just music.
The most challenging concept under the New Covenant, is that "worship" is something that the Father is seeking, and this has almost nothing to do with music.

Because the Father is seeking true worshipers, then we should understand what He means so that we can become those people He is seeking.

"But the hour is coming, and is now here, when the true worshipers will worship the Father in spirit and truth, for

the Father is seekingsuch people to worship him." (John 4:23)

Perhaps we have some preconceived ideas about what "worshiping in the spirit" means, and we are fairly convinced that we know what worshiping in truth means, for we know that the Scripture is truth. However, as much as we would like to be objective, we all have bias. Our bias is usually set to a default mode by our experience, and we simply go with that, because that is what we know. It feels comfortable.

I believe we need to go back to the Scriptures and look at them objectively, putting aside our bias and personal experiences.

We must never evaluate the Scriptures by our experience. That is the domain of deception.

But our experience should validate what the Scripture really says. If our experience does not do that, then it is time to re-evaluate what we do, and what the Scriptures really say.

The main obstacle to objective evaluation, and it is a big one, is pride.

God will resist all our efforts at adjustment, when they are based on pride.

In the Old Covenant, the people showed their worship by means of specific outward expressions.
Now in The New Covenant, we show our worship by the way we live our lives.

Worship is not contained in a particular song or a particular occasion. There is no such thing as a "worship song". If that was so, then when the song is over, we have stopped worshiping. We have come down from the altar and started living for ourselves.
No, worship is what we do all day everyday, in spirit and in truth.
The word "worship" is verb, not an adjective.

If we stop living in spirit and in truth, we stop abiding in the Vine. We stop worshiping.

Jesus' Last Teaching

During what we now call the Last Supper, the disciples would have been thinking that they were again celebrating the usual Passover meal with Jesus. They had done this before with Him.
However, Jesus knew that is was His last meal with them before He would be crucified.
A person's last words before they die are considered hugely significant, and so it was with Jesus this last time.

John records some very detailed dialogue in his Gospel during and just after the Last Supper, and as this was Jesus' last teaching time with them, it is very productive to spend time looking at that.

This last teaching of Jesus is found in chapters 13 to 17 of John's Gospel. Remember that there were no chapter or verse numbers in the original Scriptures, they were added much later.[19]

So because chapters 13 through 17 form Jesus' last teaching discourse, it is useful to read this section of Scripture as a unit.

Here is a summary of John chapters 13 to 17.

After Judas had left, Jesus starts his teaching by giving them a new commandment, then He predicts Peter's denial, tells them that He IS the Way the Truth and the Life, and tells a lot about the promise of the Holy Spirit and what He will do.

Jesus also tells them He is the Vine, tells them that the world will hate them, but that their sorrow would be turned to joy and encourages them that He has overcome the world.

Jesus finishes this His last discourse, with His incredible prayer to the Father for unity, and when that is finished, they head to the Garden of Gethsemane.

What I want to focus on here, is Jesus' teaching about the Vine.

Jesus said that He is the vine and His Father is the vinedresser. He talks about us being the branches and He talks about us being in Him. And then He talks about needing to be pruned to produce more fruit. That is the normal process for growing grape vines. Without pruning each year, the vine becomes unfruitful. The dead and unfruitful branches are cut off and burned.

Here are some things I would like to observe about this illustration from Jesus.

First, the fruit is for the Father. The fruit is not for the vine or for the branches, and it is the Father who does the pruning. He knows what He is doing, and He prunes us with Eternity in mind.

Second, the best fruit never grows on last season's branches. In fact a good vinedresser does not leave much of last season's branches on the vine at all. If he leaves them on, the fruit produced on those branches is of inferior quality. Instead, the branch is pruned right back, close to the vine.

Third, we have here an incredible picture of the fullness of the Father, Son and Holy Spirit, producing fruit in our

lives. Jesus is the vine, we are the branches, Father is the vinedresser and it makes sense to see the Holy Spirit as the life in the vine, which also flows through us.
In Galations 5:22-24 we read:
But the fruit of the Spirit is love, joy, peace, patience, kindness, goodness, faithfulness, gentleness, self-control; against such things there is no law. And those who belong to Christ Jesus have crucified the flesh with its passions and desires.
What wonderful fruit!

The fruit just grows if the branch remains in the Vine, and the fruit grows best when the branches are regularly pruned. There is no striving on the part of the branches, they simply produce fruit as long as they are in the Vine. The life of the Holy Spirit within us produces fruit for the Father.

Worship is Fruit. Fruit is Worship

In Romans 12:1-21 (the whole Chapter), we see Paul setting out some principles for what offering ourselves as a living sacrifice means and how this applies to our lives on a daily basis.

Here is what Romans 12 talks about:
Offering our lives as our reasonable sacrifice of worship,
Not being conformed to the world,
Thinking humbly of yourself and preferring one another,
Encouraging each other in our gifts,

Displaying genuine love,
Rejoicing,
Blessing others,
Showing patience,
Showing empathy and sympathy.
Not seeking your own vengeance when wronged, but ministering grace even to your enemies.

That sounds a lot like the fruit listed in Galations 5.

If we are fruitful branches, then the fruit we talked about before in Galations, will simply be illustrated by our lives, in the way Paul is describing here in Romans.
This way of living, this fruitful life, is only produced as we abide in the Vine. Our life is in Jesus. This is yielding and submitting to Him as a living sacrifice, which is our spiritual worship.

The book of James is full of practical ways in which we should be living, relating to others and serving them. The way we live has a lot to do with our worship as we have seen, but there is a perplexing passage in James 1:26 - 27.
Here, James talks about "religion", a word which occurs only a few times in the New Testament.
(The other passages are Acts 25:19, Acts 26:5, and Colossians 2:23, all with negative associations)

If anyone thinks he is religious and does not bridle his tongue but deceives his heart, this person's religion is worthless. Religion that is pure and undefiled before God the Father is this: to visit orphans and widows in their affliction, and to keep oneself unstained from the world.
(James 1:26-27)

We usually have an aversion to the word, "religion", so what is James really saying here?

Usually, religion means rituals, rules and repetition. Once we have experienced life and liberty, religion no longer describes what we have found. The clue is in the translation of the word "religion".
In the Greek, it means the manner in which a person conducts his religious worship, or what you do.[29] So it could be easily translated this way:

If anyone thinks he is a worshiper and does not bridle his tongue but deceives his heart, this person's worship is worthless. Worship that is pure and undefiled before God the Father is this: to visit orphans and widows in their affliction, and to keep oneself unstained from the world.
(James 1:26-27)

Notice that in this Scripture, James cautions us about three things: The way we talk, the way we serve, and the holiness we display in our lives.
These are elements of our worship that we should be

displaying to the world. It is what others notice about us. This is what makes us attractive to a sin-stained and damaged world.

We should be showing these things not because we need to earn points for ourselves or for our own credibility, but because others are watching the authenticity of our lives. There should be automatic fruit in our lives as we abide in the Vine, submit ourselves to His will and are willing to be pruned as the Father decides.

Jesus has also warned us that on Judgement Day, He will divide the sheep from the goats based on how we serve others. See Matthew 25:31-46.

For I was hungry and you gave me no food, I was thirsty and you gave me no drink, I was a stranger and you did not welcome me, naked and you did not clothe me, sick and in prison and you did not visit me.' (Matt 25:42-43)

Which also sounds a lot like "visiting the orphans and widows in their affliction".
This is also part of our worship. It is the New Covenant reality of the Old Covenant sacrifice.

"But the hour is coming, and is now here, when the true worshipers will worship the Father in spirit and truth, for the Father is seeking such people to worship him." (John 4:23)

In the next chapter, we will investigate the meaning of "worshiping the Father in spirit and in truth".

11. Worship in Spirit and in Truth

In order to clarify worshiping in spirit and in truth, we must understand what the Bible is referring to when we speak of "in spirit and in truth". There is much imprecise usage of these terms, especially in Charasmatic circles. Again, we should be prepared to adjust our thinking to what the Scriptures really say, even if that is uncomfortable or unfamiliar.

The subject of spirit, soul and body, becomes confusing if we do not understand the terms.

We know that man (the universal term for "mankind", or all people) has a spirit, soul and body because we are made in the image of God (three parts). In the unregenerate man, the spirit is not able to communicate with God because the Bible talks about us being "dead". (Ephesians 2:1-2 and other places)
Adam lost communication with God the day he sinned, and from then on, God never had fellowship with Adam. (Never again "walked in the garden together").

In the Bible, the word "Spirit" when used with a capital "S", refers to the person of The Holy Spirit.

When spirit is spelt with a small "s", it is referring to our own spirit, the one which is made alive when we are reborn into God's Kingdom. "S" versus "s" is extremely important to distinguish.

Jesus does not say that the Father is looking for those who worship Him with the soul.
That is the domain of our emotions and our feelings. Unfortunately, this is the domain in which most of our "worship" is focused. We mistake feelings and emotions for the prompting of the Holy Spirit, so we actually miss out on worshiping the Father.

It will be useful to spend a little time on clarifying the role of our spirit, soul and body.

Here is a quote from Andrew Murray, which is a good summary of the three aspects of man: spirit, soul and body.

"In the history of man's creation we read, 'The Lord God formed man of the dust of the ground'—thus was his body made— 'and breathed into his nostrils the breath' or spirit 'of life': thus his spirit came from God; 'and man became a living soul.' The spirit quickening the body made man a living soul, a living person with the consciousness of himself. The soul was the meeting-place, the point of union between body and spirit. Through the body, man the living soul, stood related to the external world of sense; could influence it, or be influenced by it. Through the spirit he stood related to the spiritual world and the Spirit of God, whence he had his origin, and could be the recipient and the minister of its life and power. Standing thus midway between two worlds, belonging to both, the soul had the power of determining itself, of choosing or refusing the objects by which it was surrounded, and to which it stood related.

In the constitution of these three parts of man's nature, the spirit, as linking him with the Divine, was the highest; the body, connecting him with the sensible and animal, the lowest.

In the intermediate stands the soul, partaker of the nature of the others, the bond that unites them, and through which they act on each other. Its work, as the central power, is to maintain them in their due relation; to keep the body, as the lowest, in subjection to the spirit, and itself to receive through the spirit as the higher."

Andrew Murray, The Spirit of Christ. Fort Washington, Pa., Christian Literature Crusade, 1964. Note C: The Place of the Indwelling, p.227-228.

The following diagram helps to illustrate the way Murray is describing the relationship between spirit, soul and body. Always have in mind "S" versus "s".

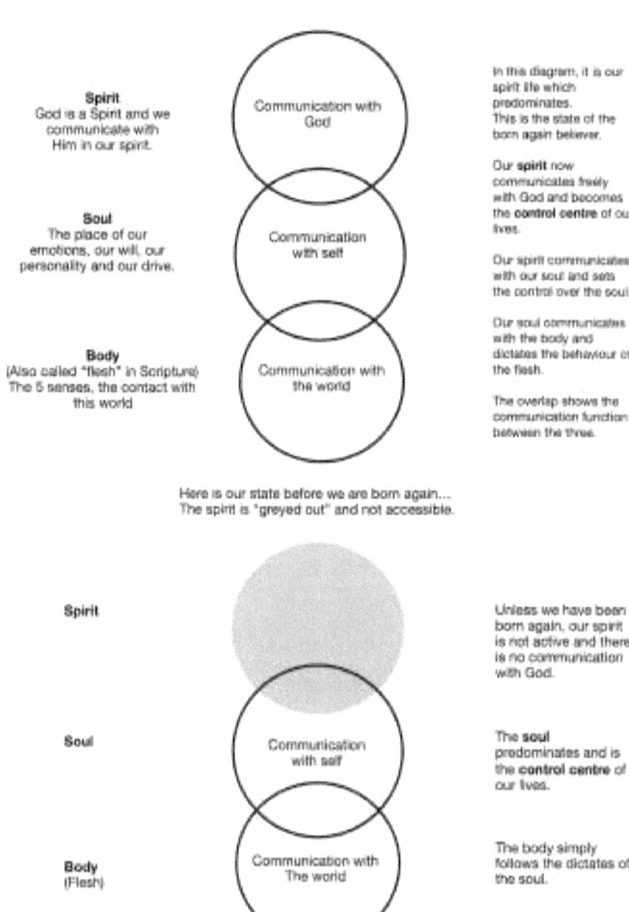

Let's look at 1 Cor 15:45

So also it is written, "The first man Adam became a living soul"; the last Adam became a life-giving spirit. (1 Cor 15:45 NASB)

Paul says here that the first Adam became a living soul. The soul is alive. It has its own life, therefore it enables man to think, feel, imagine and love. This refers to the way in which which Adam operated. Then Paul continues with: "the last Adam (Jesus) became a life-giving spirit." This Scripture is worthy of close attention, for it is showing plainly, the difference between our soul and our spirit.

Notice too in John 4, and this is very important, that when Jesus says the Father is seeking people to worship Him in spirit and in truth, (John 4:23) there is a lower case "s" spirit. This is our spirit, our reborn and in-contact-with-God spirit. Not the Holy Spirit.

The different operation of our spirit and the operation of the soul are seen here.

Our soul is alive and has life in itself.

Our spirit works in co-operation with the Spirit of God - The Holy Spirit.

The soul is itself living, yet it cannot make others live. But the Holy Spirit is not only living, He can also give others life. Only the Holy Spirit is capable of quickening people into life. The soul, no matter how strong it is, cannot impart life to others. "It is the Spirit," says the Lord, "that gives life; the flesh is of no value".

Because our spirit is in communication with the Holy Spirit, we are able to co-operate with Him in bringing people to Jesus. This indeed is an incredible privilege. But we must be very careful, never to operate in the soul or the flesh. Our actions are polluted if we do.

It is the Spirit who gives life (the Holy Spirit) ; the flesh is no help at all. The words that I have spoken to you are spirit (our spirit) and life. (John 6:63)

Worship in spirit.

The soul does not give life, but it draws to itself.

Unfortunately, this is evident in many of our church services, especially in Blackbox Worship. Soulish manipulation is ultimately the realm of witchcraft. Gradually, the music has to become more and more majestic, more appealing, we need more tech, more lights and more sound, bigger auditoriums and more people. But this only results in operating more in the soul realm which we mistake for "Worship in the Holy Spirit". This is a huge mistake. This is the realm of the soul - of feelings and emotions, it is not worshiping "in the spirit" as the Father desires.

Jesus puts it this way…
Truly, truly, I say to you, unless a grain of wheat falls into the earth and dies, it remains alone; but if it dies, it bears much fruit. Whoever loves his life loses it, and whoever hates his life in this world will keep it for eternal life. (John 12:24-25)

"Losing your life" means losing your soul life.
The word "life" here in this verse in the original Greek[30]points to the soul, meaning our emotions, feelings, desires, affections and aversions.
If we live in the soul, we will lose our lives. If we put the soul aside and subjugate it to the spirit, we will gain our life - and then we also enrich our soul life. Our soul life is like that grain of wheat. If it sits on a table, then ten years later it will still be a grain of wheat. But if it is planted and "dies", it will produce much more grain.
Worshiping in the spirit means that the soul has no control in how we worship.

However, it is still possible to live from the soul as a believer. We always have a choice. We can ignore the promptings of the Holy Spirit and instead be led by our habits, experience, emotions and feelings. Or we can, as Paul phrases it, crucify the flesh and die to our own desires.

Our responsibility is to die daily. If we die, we will produce much fruit. As we are pruned, we produce more fruit. Pruning (cutting off, dying) is necessary to produce fruit for the Father.
This is true worship, and it is done in the spirit, not in the soul.
The Holy Spirit never utilises the power of our soul, even though our soul is a powerful force. The Holy Spirit brings us to the point of laying down our life - the soul life

- every single day. God is so good to us!
This is worshiping in the spirit.

Here is John 5:19…
So Jesus said to them, "Truly, truly, I say to you, the Son can do nothing of his own accord, but only what he sees the Father doing. For whatever the Father does, that the Son does likewise.

Jesus put aside his own will, put aside his own emotions and feelings (his soul), and made a conscious decision to only do what He saw the Father do. He completely subjugated His will to the Father's will. Jesus was fully led by the spirit - his own human spirit - in co-operation with the Holy Spirit.

<u>Jesus never operated in the power of His soul.</u>

He never emotionally manipulated His disciples.
He never used crowd control techniques.
He never used His powers of persuasion or oratory.
He never used the power of His personality to achieve a desired result.
He never complained or suffered lack.
He never did what He wanted, but only what He saw the Father do.

This was Jesus' demonstration to us, of real worship. Jesus laid down his life because it is what the Father wanted him to do.
Abraham did this with Isaac, when God asked him to sacrifice his son.
The women with the expensive perfume did this too. They poured out a whole year's salary on Jesus as a huge sacrifice. Everything they had.
We can also do this, in whatever capacity the Lord requires of us, in the power of the Holy Spirit.

Romans 12:1 is illustrated in practice here, even to death. Our illustration and example is as always, Jesus.
Is this not what Jesus said to the Father in the Garden of Gethsemane before he went to the cross?

Jesus knew what was coming.
He had known it for a long time, perhaps all his life.

"Nevertheless, not my will, but yours"*(Luke 22:42),*

is probably the most powerful statement of submission to the Father's will ever recorded.

This dear Saints, I believe, is the essence of true worship, the worship the Father is seeking.
Here is a main focus of the New Testament, which contains

a comprehensive description of our worship to the Father.

Romans 12:1 is the New Covenant fulfilment of Abraham's sacrifice of Isaac.
In a very real sense, Isaac was also a living sacrifice, in Abraham's estimation.
God's call on Abraham's life was no more significant than the call the Father has on our own life. But God wants us to see, and to demonstrate to Him that we really know, that there is nothing more important in our life than our worship of Him.
Worshiping Him is more important even the promises and calling on our life that God has made. But we need to show that is the reality in our own life.

This is the living sacrifice that Paul is urging us to present to the Father.
This is worship in the spirit.

Our part in the whole process is to be fully yielded, day by day in a life surrendered to His service. This is true worship, and that is what our Lord Jesus is going to be looking for when He says to some on that day, "Well done, good and faithful servant".

Our life begins in the Spirit, our life is empowered by the Spirit, and our life is completed in the Spirit. No wonder the Father is seeking this kind of person; the kind of person whose will is completely and unconditionally surrendered to the will of the Father, the person who is led

by and filled with, the Holy Spirit.
Only then can we find the fulfilment in life which we so desperately seek. Look not to any other place.

Jesus, our elder brother, the first of many brethren, modelled this perfectly for us so that we may know the way. He is the Way, the Truth and the Life. Being a true disciple of Jesus means becoming like the Master in every aspect.
It means abandoning our will for His will in our lives. It means knowing Him in a very personal way, and becoming transformed into His image by the power of the Holy Spirit.
This is not an automatic process, but depends on us being willing to be pruned and fashioned according to the Father's will.
When Jesus came to Earth as a man, He got His own body and He got His own soul and He got His own spirit. He learned to worship the Father in his own spirit and in truth.

Jesus demonstrated worship in every way, because He was willing to submit His will to the Father. And yet He too had to learn obedience, just like we do.

Obedience is a key ingredient of our worship.
We can only learn obedience by obeying. It is a skill that we learn by doing, just like riding a bicycle. You can not

learn to ride a bicycle by reading a book, it is something you have to do. You need to experience it.

That is why Jesus had to learnobedience. He had never had to experience doing that before.
Although he was a son, he learned obedience through what he suffered. (Hebrews 5:8)

There is a lot of teaching in the New Testament about suffering, and we will not dig too deeply into that here. However, Jesus says we will suffer and be persecuted in this life. Peter teaches on suffering, (as also does Paul.)
Suffering makes us strong, and produces the strongest of all relationship bonds.
Which is why in part we are privileged to be able, in a microscopic way, to share in the sufferings of Jesus.

Beloved, do not be surprised at the fiery trial when it comes upon you to test you, as though something strange were happening to you. But rejoice insofar as you share Christ's sufferings, that you may also rejoice and be glad when his glory is revealed.
(1 Peter 4:12-13)

Testing is not God's tool for crushing us. Testing is part of His process for making us strong, for making sure we are fully equipped and ready. He is preparing us for Eternity.
Jesus is our Master, our Lord, our Defender, our Provider,

our Source, our beginning and our endpoint. He is the one who perfectly modelled what it means to worship the Father in spirit and in truth.

Suffering is not a strange thing, it is necessary if we are to progress deeper in God.

Suffering is part of sacrifice. Embrace suffering dear Saints, because God is faithful. He deals with us from the perspective of Eternity. We can not see that, but we can trust Him because of His character.

Jesus never calls us to do something that He did not first show us how to do. He also gave us the power of the Holy Spirit, who enables us to do anything to which He calls us. And we are called to be His disciples.

Jesus' early disciples modelled that for us, the Saints through history have modelled that for us, and there are also present day saints who model that for us.
This is the fulfilment of the picture of worship we see under the Mosaic Covenant in the Old Testament.
We have arrived at the place the travel brochure informed us about. This is Jesus' kingdom and this is where He wants us to live.
The old has gone, the fulfilment is here.

Here is a major theme of Paul's teaching and other letters in the New Testament.
The reality of our life as a disciple of Jesus is a demonstration of our worship to the Father.
We are called to make worshiping God the focus of our whole lives.

May this demonstration be our life, because The Father is seeking such to worship Him. Those who will worship Him in (our) spirit.

Worship in truth.
We have looked in detail at worshiping in the spirit and what that means.
Now let us look at worshiping in truth.

"But the hour is coming, and is now here, when the true worshipers will worship the Father in spirit and truth,for the Father is seeking such people to worship him." (John 4:23)

Pilate said "What is truth?" (John 18:38)

This is a debate that university lecturers and professors and other intellectuals engage in at great length, without resolve.
They try to find truth without Jesus, and that is a futile pursuit.

If what we do and the way we live and act does not line up with what Jesus says in the Bible, we do not live in truth.

The truth is Jesus, because He says simply, "I am the Way and the Truth and the Life".
We can only worship in truth if we know the Truth. Jesus is the Truth, so we must get to know Him.

Because Jesus is the Way, we know that the direction He sets is certain to be the correct one. There is only one way to God, not many.
Because Jesus is the Truth,we must diligently strive to understand everything Jesus said. Otherwise we do not know the Truth.
Because Jesus is the Life,He is the only one who can show us what it means to be
dead to ourselves and alive to Christ.

Let us focus on truth for a moment, because Jesus wants us to worship the Father in truth.
We know that the law was given through Moses, but grace and truth came through Jesus. (John 1:17) Everything Jesus said and did brought the truth. The things He said about Himself from the Old Testament and the things He said about Himself in the New Testament, are truth.
Everything He said.
And that excludes any other belief or teaching that is presented as "truth", because Jesus said "I" am the Truth.

He Himself is the Truth. Jesus is not pointing the way to some truth, He isthe Truth.

We also know that Jesus is the Word. This is the name that John gives Jesus in the beginning of his Gospel. *"In the beginning was the Word…" (John 1:1)*
The "Word" with a capital letter like that, indicates that this is Jesus' name before He became man and lived as Jesus on Earth. John knew that Jesus had always existed with the Father and the Holy Spirit, so he finds a way to describe what He was called before His birth.

"Word" is translated from the Greek word "Logos".[31]
Logos has a breadth and depth of meaning that John's readers would have understood, but that depth escapes us if we do not know the Greek language. Fortunately for most of us who do not know Greek, there are many resources at our fingertips to unlock the meaning.
The plainest meaning is "the written word", which means the written text of scripture as we have it in our Bibles.
However, we get our English word, "logic" from logos and so we see another depth here. Logos (the logic) is also the root of other English words such as biology, theology, geology, palaeontology, radiology, psychology. Used in this way, it shows "the study of things", or "the knowledge associated with this field". It is the sum of knowledge about those subjects, the reason why everything works that way.

Thus, "biology" is the study of life and the reasons behind how it works, "theology" is the study of God, "geology" is the study of the Earth, and so on.

When John calls Jesus the Word, he is saying that Jesus is and always was, the reason behind everything.
We also know the same thing from Colossians where Paul focuses on everything Jesus is and has done.

Jesus transferred us into His kingdom;
He is the image of God;
Everything was made by Him, Through Him and for Him;
Everything is sustained and held together by Him; (if Jesus stopped sustaining us for an instant of time, everything would go back to the nothing that it was before creation - The Void.)
(Colossians 1:13-23)

Jesus is not just "the reason for the season". That is superficial.
Jesus is the Logos, He is the Word, He is the reason whyabout everything.
Jesus is Truth and the reason why, in every way about everything.
Jesus never did or said anything that was not Truth.

We must be constantly in the Word, and in the word.
We must be in Jesus, and in the Bible.

You cannot separate the person of Jesus from the written word, the Bible.

He is to be found in all the pages of Scripture, He is to be found in the slightest sighing of a breeze, He is to be found in the most brilliant sunset, He is to be found in the majesty and power of a massive thunderstorm.

Jesus the person (God), can be understood by the things He has made (Romans 1:20), but they are a minuscule fraction of the actual person.

When people in the Bible actually saw the real Jesus in His resurrected power and glory and splendour, they were terrified and overcome with fear.[32]Let not anybody say they have seen Jesus, unless they have also felt His fearsome power and blinding beauty and crushing might. He is not just a man anymore.
He exists in his Glorified, Resurrected body and is clothed in Splendour. Our natural bodies of dust actually can not survive in the full presence of His Glory.
If anyone claims to have seen Jesus, and responds to His manifest glorified presence in a casual way, we know they did not meet the real Jesus.

When Jesus comes back as Lord and conquering King at the end of days, those who do not know Him will be overcome with intense fear like never before. His appearance will frighten people so badly that they will

faint, or their hearts will fail.[33] His word will scatter His enemies and shatter their futile defences.
Just His word will do that!

He created the universe by the word of His mouth. It obeyed Him and it was so.
He will also destroy His enemies with the word of His mouth. It will be so.

We worship the Father in truth as we submit our lives to our Kingly, Glorious, Resurrected Jesus with this perspective.
How could we possibly not want to submit to the supreme Lord, when we understand who He really is?
Jesus is the Truth. Do not look anywhere else.

Here are some things that Scripture says about truth:

By this we know love, that he laid down his life for us, and we ought to lay down our lives for the brothers. But if anyone has the world's goods and sees his brother in need, yet closes his heart against him, how does God's love abide in him? Little children, let us not love in word or talk but in deed and in truth. By this we shall know that we are of the truth and reassure our heart before him; (1 John 3:16-19)

The elder to the elect lady and her children, whom I love in truth, and not only I, but also all who know the truth, because of the truth that abides in us and will be with us forever: (2 John 1-2)

The elder to the beloved Gaius, whom I love in truth. (3 John 1)

Here are some questions as we end this section on truth, and this chapter on worship in our daily life.

Are we constrained by the Word of God, or by the traditions of men?
We say we hold the Bible as the foremost authority in our thinking, but how much time do we spend reading and studying our Bibles? If it really is your priority, let it show.
How well do we know the Word (Jesus)?
How well do we know Jesus (The Word)?
We know our priorities by the way we spend our "spare" time. What does our spare time tell us?
If what we think conflicts with what the Word says, do we just ignore it and say it does not apply here, or do we humbly adjust what we think?
Do we dig deep into the substance of God's Word, or do we just go with the internet "verse of the day"…?
Would we be willing to go to jail for what we believe?
Are we prepared to die for what we believe?

12. Worship In Our Future

We have seen that worship as described by the New Covenant, is not a form or a formula.
Neither is worship linked to music as a medium or a mechanism or a necessary ingredient of worship.

Worship is the way we live before God. He wants us to please Him, and He wants us to honour Him with our lives. Our expensive, redeemed lives.

The Father prunes and shapes our lives according to His infinite wisdom and righteousness, always from the perspective of Eternity.
But unlike the natural vine, our Heavenly Vinedresser seeks our permission and co-operation.
It is our decision to abide in the Vine, and this is the only way we produce real fruit. The fruit that is worship, the fruit that comes from our life in Jesus.

…for the Father is seeking such to worship Him." (John 4:23)

However, our enemy, the devil, is also seeking people who will worship him.
"And he(the devil) *said to him*(Jesus), *'all these I will give you if you will fall down and worship me'." (Matthew 4:9)*

But Jesus completely disarmed and dismissed the devil in His wilderness temptations, with the Word;
'Be gone, Satan! For it is written, 'You shall worship the Lord your God and him only shall you serve.' Then the devil left Him…" (Matthew 4:10)
This was the beginning of the devil's harassment of Jesus, to try to see if he could get Jesus to bow down and worship him. The devil constantly plagued Jesus with temptations until Jesus died. The devil tempted Jesus "in every respect as we are".
But the enemy also failed in every respect with Jesus.
However, the devil does not give up easily. He is always trying to seduce us into worshiping anything except God.

For we do not have a high priest who is unable to sympathise with our weaknesses, but one who in every respect has been tempted as we are, yet without sin. (Hebrews 4:15)

If the the enemy cannot trick us into worshiping him directly with satanic things like ouija boards, seances and satanic rituals, he will try to seduce us into worshiping idols. An idol can be something man-made or even something God has made.

In Romans Chapter 1:20-25 we see that Paul warns us against worshiping anything else; worshiping the creation rather than the creator.

… Claiming to be wise, they became fools, and exchanged the glory of the immortal God for images resembling mortal man and birds and animals and creeping things.
Therefore God gave them up in the lusts of their hearts to impurity, to the dishonoring of their bodies among themselves, because they exchanged the truth about God for a lie and worshiped and served the creature rather than the Creator,who is blessed forever! Amen. (Romans 1:22-25, Emphasis mine.)

This worship could be anything - education, light and sound, science and nature, knowledge, marriage and children, family, politics, music, drugs, alcohol, sex and so on.
These are the obvious ones, but the enemy is subtle and cunning. There can be idols of even things that are "good", like church leaders, music, church organisations, charity organisations and clubs, fitness and even your own body. These are all false worship, and anything that is false will produce distraction, despair and eventually distruction in our life.

You know the thing we are worshiping, by understanding what occupies the main priority in our life.
If your priority is serving God, then you are a person the

Father is seeking.
This is also why Jesus said in Matt 6:33,
"But seek first the kingdom of God and his righteousness, and all these things will be added to you."

The first thing in your life must be the Kingdom Of God, if you are to really become a worshiper.
We can think that we are putting the Kingdom first, but there still may be something or someone who has the first place. A Pastor or Leader or an organisation, can subtly hold a higher place in a person's thinking than the Word Of God. Such a person relies on and will refer to, the Pastor or Leader or organisational doctrines in preference to the Word.

It is almost as if the Word holds no authority in their life. Some often unknowingly, revere the words of the Pastor as equivalent to the Word of God. Actually, by their actions they demonstrate that they would believe what the Pastor says, in preference to what the Word says.

We must be like the Bereans who constantly researched and double checked everything against the Scriptures.

Now these Jews were more noble than those in Thessalonica; they received the word with all eagerness, examining the Scriptures daily to see if these things were so. (Acts 17:11)

Remember the Fifth Column. We must actively and continuously guard against deception.

Here is how God describes worship in the Old Covenant:
"When the LORD your God cuts off before you the nations whom you go in to dispossess, and you dispossess them and dwell in their land, take care that you be not ensnared to follow them, after they have been destroyed before you, and that you do not inquire about their gods, saying, 'How did these nations serve their gods?--that I also may do the same.'
You shall not worship the LORD your God in that way, for every abominable thing that the LORD hates they have done for their gods, for they even burn their sons and their daughters in the fire to their gods. "Everything that I command you, you shall be careful to do. You shall not add to it or take from it."(Deuteronomy 12:29-32 Emphasis mine)

Jesus wants this type and shadow of Old Covenant worship, to be real in our own lives, now that He has established the New Covenant.

Here is how God describes worship in the New Covenant:
Love not the world, neither the things that are in the world. If any man love the world, the love of the Father is not in him. For all that is in the world, the lust of the flesh, and the lust of the eyes, and the pride of life, is not of the Father, but is of the world. (1 John 2:15-16)

In the New Covenant, we are empowered by and guided by the Holy Spirit. We have a heart that is flesh and not stone, a heart that can be responsive to the call of the Holy Spirit. We are now able to live a life which is pleasing to God.
True worship, reasonable worship, the logical worship that we should bring in response, is to offer ourselves as a living sacrifice. (Romans 12:1)

This is the New Covenant reality of the Old Covenant type.
This is what the Father is seeking - those who will worship Him in spirit and truth.

We have seen that real worship is an action towards God, which is mostly not linked to music.
Most of the acts of worship in the Old Testament did not involve music at all.
Music in the New Covenant is almost completely absent, as are the "Worship Leader" and the "Worship Ministry". There is no such thing as a "worship" song.

We need to re-define our idea of real worship according to The Word Of God, not according to our experience.
If we never do this, we may never find the reality of what the Father is seeking.
Jesus says *"true worshiperswill worship the Father in spirit and in*

truth, for the Father is seeking such people to worship Him." (John 4:23)

If we use music and songs as the main part of our "worship", we are most impoverished indeed, because not only have we have missed out on worshiping the Father, we have completely misunderstood the reality of real worship.
Abraham, Job and David did not need any songs or music to express their worship to the Father.
Jesus, Peter, Paul, John and other disciples did not need music to express their worship and devotion to the Father.

"Christian" music, and the modern "Praise and Worship" marketing machine, are a huge distraction from the real worship that the Father is seeking.
The Father is not seeking Blackbox Worship or a setlist of songs from CCLI, or an hour long You Tube clip of someone's idea of "worship songs".

The New Testament is our worship manual.
It is a manual for living our lives as God wants, in complete and continual surrender to His will, as an expression of offering ourselves as a living sacrifice.

This is how Jesus lived. He modelled for us what it means to be a living sacrifice.

The Father knows we are weak and frail, and that worshiping Him renews our strength.

Yet those who wait for the LORD Will gain new strength; They will mount up with wings like eagles, They will run and not get tired, They will walk and not become weary.
(Isaiah 40:31, NASB)

Waiting upon (or "for") the Lord, trusting Him, expecting Him to guide and lead us, is part of our worship towards God. It acknowledges Him as our source and our purpose. This gives us new strength and renews our vision.
He made us that way, we are designed and built to worship.

In the Old Covenant, they had specific times, places and actions of worship.
In the New Covenant, we worship by the way we live.
If we live according to the Word in (our) spirit and in truth, we are worshiping the Father.

But God knows that in our weak and sinful, unredeemed state, it is impossible to worship Him at all. In our former unredeemed state we defaulted to worshiping in the enemy's kingdom, because that is where we used to live. We actually worshipped the enemy in our fallen state.

For he has rescued us from the kingdom of darkness and transferred us into the Kingdom of his dear Son,

(Colossians 1:13 NLT)

God provided a way of redeeming us and restoring us to the relationship with Him that He designed from the beginning. He rescued us from the kingdom of darkness and placed us in the Kingdom of Jesus.

If you do not yet know for sure if you have been translated from the Kingdom of Darkness and brought into the Kingdom Of Jesus, the Good News is right here.

This is the Gospel, how we become translated into the Kingdom Of Jesus:
First, acknowledge that you are indeed a sinner and the penalty of sin is death.
Second, understand that Jesus has paid the death penalty for you.
Third, repent and turn away from your sin.
Fourthly, get baptised - real baptism by immersion in water.
Fifthly, ask Jesus to baptise you in the Holy Spirit. You need His power to live this life.

The rest of the story is about living in the amazing life He has given us, in the power of the Holy Spirit.

See contact information in the Appendix if you would like more information.[34]

God gave us Jesus who paid our restoration price.
He sent us the Holy Spirit who gives us the power to live as He requires, and to be able to share that freedom with others.
Then He says "well done, good and faithful servant", after solving the problem and giving us everything we need.

We created the problem, He solved it on His own initiative at great expense, gave us the ability to live as He wants, then congratulates us for doing it!
Not just that, but He has designed a place for us to live eternally with Him, which is actually beyond our wildest imagination.

This is what we celebrate when we celebrate the Lord's Supper together

How little we deserve His favour!
What a wonderful God we serve, and what a wonderful place He has prepared for us!

May we offer ourselves a living sacrifice, as our logical response in worship to the Lord. May the Lord consume our lives, like the sacrifice was consumed on the altar in

the Old Covenant.
May the fragrance of that offering become the thing which draws others out of the kingdom of darkness and into the kingdom of Jesus.

Let us become the people whom the Father is seeking.

"But the hour is coming, and is now here, when the true worshipers will worship the Father in spirit and truth, for the Father is seeking such people to worship him." (John 4:23)

May the Lord bless you
as you seek to become someone
who worships the Father
in spirit and in truth

Appendix

(Internet references are correct at the time of publishing and may change.
They are a simple guide to your own research and are not necessarily the only sources.)

1. Hatred between the Jews and the Samaritans
https://bible.org/illustration/hatred-between-jews-and-samaritans

2. John 4:26

3. Jesus rebukes Scribes and Pharisees. Matt 12:33-50, Mark 3:31-35, Luke 8:19-21

4. Principle of First Mention
https://www.compellingtruth.org/law-of-first-mention.html
Here are some "firsts":
Salvation: Gen 3:15b,
Baptism: The Flood is a figure of baptism (1 Peter 3:20-21)
The Bride of Christ: Gen 2:24

The Church: Gen 12:2-3 (all nations to be blessed)
The Second coming: Gen 2:1-3 (Which is the Sabbath rest)
The Trinity: Genesis 1:1-2

5.Satan confronts God about Job. Job 1: 6-12

6. Job's Calamities Job 1:13-19

7. David, a man after God's own heart. Acts 13:22, 1 Sam 13:14,

8. Cost to build Solomon's Temple.
https://www.answers.com/Q/How_much_would_King_Solomon's_Temple_cost_to_build_today

9. Distance from Obed-Edom's house to Jerusalem
https://www.answers.com/Q/How_far_is_it_from_Obed-Edom's_house_to_Jerusalem
https://emmausroadministries.international/2021/08/25/why-did-the-oxen-stumble/

10. Resources on Praise
https://www.intimacywithgod.com/2019/08/27/praise-is-a-weapon-for-spiritual-warfare/

Also Find Prison To Praise by Merlin Carothers on Amazon and other places. Look for the 1970 version.

11. Notes on St Augustine
https://www.cliffsnotes.com/literature/s/st-augustines-confessions/st-augustine-biography
https://robertcliftonrobinson.com/2020/05/23/the-old-testament-is-the-new-testament-concealed-the-new-testament-is-the-old-testament-revealed/

12. Was Jesus Crucified where Abraham offered Isaac?
https://messianic-revolution.com/22-5-was-yeshuas-sacrifice-also-on-mt-moriah/
https://www.sermoncentral.com/sermon-illustrations/83602/parallels-between-isaac-and-jesus-by-dr-larry-petton
This is possible, but because the Bible does not state that explicitly, then we can not be 100% sure.

13. Ancient Traditional Jewish wedding customs.
https://www.biblestudytools.com/commentaries/revelation/related-topics/the-jewish-wedding-analogy.html
https://luke1041.blogspot.com/2012/06/lessons-from-alabaster-box.html

14. Not In Our Own Strength

Matt 6:24-26, 1Cor 15:31, Eph 4:22-24, Gal5 5:24, Rom 8:13-14, Eph 6:10, 1 Tim 1:12

15. Jesus Rejoiced

Greek agalliaō (Strongs G21) ἀγαλλιάω agalliáō, ag-al-lee-ah'-o; from agan (much) and G242;
properly, to jump for joy, i.e. exult:—be (exceeding) glad, with exceeding joy, rejoice (greatly).

16. The last song Jesus sang

https://hallel.info/psalm-113-118-the-hallel-and-the-passover/

17. Psalms, Hymns, Spiritual Songs

Greek: Psalmos G5568, Hymnos G5215, Pneumatikos G4152
See Strongs references in Blue Letter Bible

18. Angels didn't sing at Jesus' birth

Luke 2:13

19. Origin Of Our Biblical Numbering System

Chapter numbers were added by Stephen Langton, Archbishop of Canterbury in 1227.

The Old Testament had verse numbers added by a Jewish Rabbi, Nathan, in 1448.
The New Testament verse numbers were added by Robert Estienne, in 1555.
See:
https://www.gotquestions.org/divided-Bible-Chapters-verses.html
https://en.wikipedia.org/wiki/Chapters_and_verses_of_the_Bible

20. Unlocking The Bible by David Pawson
The book is Available on Amazon, Book Depository and other places
https://www.amazon.com/Unlocking-Bible-Unique-Overview-Whole/dp/1943852650
The hard copy is highly recommended, as the charts and graphics are all included.
The videos of this series are also currently available on You Tube. Look up "David Pawson Unlocking The Bible."

21. In-depth teaching on the Covenants
The basis of this teaching is from David Pawson, Biblical Covenants (in 3 parts)
www.youtube.com/watch?v=8AEHKif3-Ts

22. The life is in the blood
Leviticus 17:11

23. Berith
http://ecclesia.org/truth/contracts.html

24. The law was a shadow of things to come
Hebrews 10:1

25. How Music Manipulates Us(Easy to find with a simple search for "music and emotions")
1. You are being manipulated - Supermarket buying
https://techfeatured.com/12146/youre-being-manipulated-how-music-affects-your-buying-habits
2. Empathy manipulation
https://pubmed.ncbi.nlm.nih.gov/22292000/
3. Music and movies
http://www.cardiffsciscreen.co.uk/article/music-and-emotional-manipulation-movies
4. Sensory Marketing - Berkley Political Review
https://bpr.berkeley.edu/2021/05/29/sensory-marketing-when-music-makes-you-buy/
5. A Church Music Leader explains how you are manipulated
www.youtube.com/watch?v=XoaknMByfRs
6. The Dark reality of the Christian music industry
www.youtube.com/watch?v=IEbyzZE5nzA
7. Church Music Is Designed To Influence You
www.youtube.com/watch?v=7btz0ocXDeg

26. Soaking Music.
Caution: Not recommended for longer than a few seconds.

This music changes your brain patterns. See Appendix 25
1. From Bethel
www.youtube.com/watch?v=Xx1MjhzKcYw
2. New Age
www.youtube.com/watch?v=LV7SgbEi48Y
3. From Elevation
www.youtube.com/watch?v=T2Zda2fuey8

27. God gave Moses the 10 commandments and the plans for the Tabernacle
Exodus 24:12 to Exodus 31:18

28. CCLI
This is the licensing organisation for songs used in churches. The church pays a subscription fee to CCLI in order to use their copyright material.

29. Religion
The Greek is thrēskeia. (Strongs G2356) religious worship, external, that which consists of ceremonies, religious discipline, religion

30. Life
The Greek is psychē (Strongs G5590) It means the soul life of animals or men. Referring to the seat of our feelings, desires, affections, aversions. It is mostly translated "soul" in the Bible. We get our word psychology from psyche.

31. Word

The Greek is logos (Strongs G3056)

Note: A Greek philosopher named Heraclitus first used the term Logos around 600 B.C. to designate the divine reason or plan which coordinates a changing universe. Cambridge Dictionary of Philosophy (2nd ed): Heraclitus, 1999.

This is the definition that was probably in the minds of the readers to whom John was writing the Gospel.

32. Some Appearances of the Risen, Glorified Jesus

Paul on the Road to Damascus. Acts 9:1-9

John. Revelation 1:12-18

33. Mens Hearts Failing them for fear

Luke 21:26. It will be fearful time for those who do not know the Lord.

34. Contact Information

Email: davidcmiles@protonmail.com

You Tube: https://www.youtube.com/channel/UC_tezzndKAxTVKLBASqwCvw?view_as=subscriber

(The You Tube channel has more information about Water Baptism, Baptism in The Holy Spirit, some songs and an eBook read by Alison).

www.ingramcontent.com/pod-product-compliance
Lightning Source LLC
LaVergne TN
LVHW050409160726
843469LV00041B/1007

* 9 7 8 9 3 5 6 1 0 4 5 2 5 *